ONLY IN
VIRGINIA

ONLY IN
VIRGINIA

*The Unique History,
Humor, and Heart
of the Old Dominion*

CARRIE SHOOK
and
ROBERT L. SHOOK

A Perigee Book

Perigee Books
are published by
The Putnam Publishing Group
200 Madison Avenue
New York, NY 10016

Library of Congress Cataloging-in-Publication Data

Shook, Carrie, date.
Only in Virginia: the unique history, humor, and heart of the Old
    Dominion / by Carrie Shook and Robert L. Shook.
        p.   cm.
    1. Virginia—Description and travel—1981–   —Guide-books.
    2. Virginia—Miscellanea.   I. Shook, Robert L., date.
II. Title.
    ISBN 0-399-51556-9
    F224.3.S56   1989   89-37563 CIP
    917.5504′43—dc20

Printed in the United States of America

1   2   3   4   5   6   7   8   9   10

Acknowledgments

We would like to thank the following people for their tremendous contributions: Brett Battles, Gary Berdeaux, Christian Cevaer, Ron Clark, Liz Conover, Cynthia Conte, Patty Fletcher, Anil Gangolli, James F. Garrett, Joseph D. Grandstaff, Elaine W. Hall, Karen Hedelt, Elisabeth Jaffe, Ken Kipps, Chris Korleski, Warren Lawrence, Michael Anne Lynn, Bruce Meyer, Jeff Meyer, Jon Meyer, Matt Meyer, Nancy Meyer, Charlotte Moyler, Jim Moyler, Anne Johnson Myers, Joe Myers, Debby Padget, Jason Robert Plummer, Kara Read, Mike Shook, R. J. Shook, Becky Smith, C. Vaughan Stanley, Annie Bell Taylor, Winston B. Tolley, David Tornes, Millie Travis, Hester L. Waterfield, James E. Wootton, and Al Zuckerman.

We would also like to thank the chambers of commerce throughout the state that gave us their valuable assistance; and Ash Lawn–Highland, Barter Theatre, Bexley Public Library, City of Virginia Beach Tourism Development Division, College of William and Mary, Colonial Williamsburg Foundation, Endless Caverns, Historic Country Inns, Historic Fredericksburg Department of Tourism, Jamestown-Yorktown Foundation, Luray Caverns, Michie Tavern, Monticello, Museum of American Frontier Culture, Natural Bridge Village, Robert E. Lee Memorial Association, Stonewall Jackson House, and Virginia Division of Tourism.

Special Acknowledgment

We would like to thank our editors, Lindley Boegehold and Tina Isaac, for their creative force and dedicated effort.

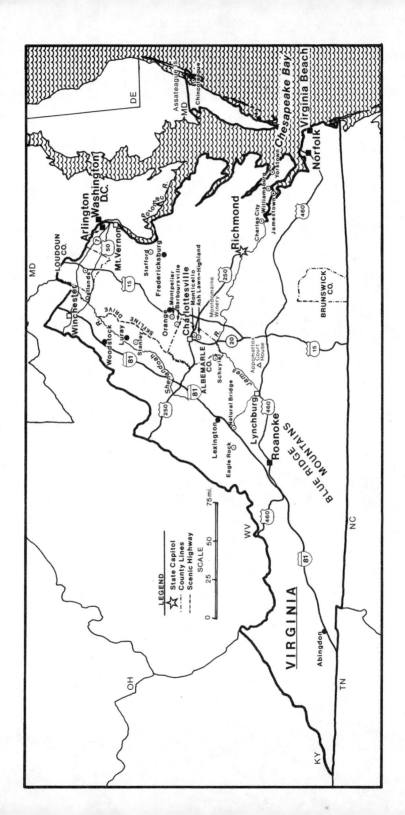

Contents

Introduction

The motto "Virginia Is for Lovers" does not just represent the state's romantic appeal but captures the allure of its golden beaches, tall mountains, and deep caverns. Then too, Virginia is for those who love history and the patriots who made American independence a reality.

An incredible wealth of history comes from this state. Within Virginia's borders are the early colonies of Jamestown, Yorktown, and Williamsburg. The first Thanksgiving was celebrated in Virginia, even before the Pilgrims landed at Plymouth! Visits to historical sites such as Mount Vernon, Monticello, and the Arlington National Cemetery are like walking through the pages of a history book.

Virginia is the birthplace of our country, site of the first English settlement and home of our forefathers, including George Washington, Thomas Jefferson, James Madison, and James Monroe. Many of the nation's great military leaders were Virginians, among them Washington, Stonewall Jackson, Robert E. Lee, and George Marshall. Virginia continued its military tradition as it played a major role in Navy history. In July 1917, the Norfolk Naval Base was commissioned; today it is the largest naval installation in the world.

This land is blessed by nature. Once the American frontier, the majestic Shenandoah Valley and its crystal caverns offer an ancient history tracing back centuries to American

11

Indians. The Skyline Drive along the crest of the Blue Ridge Mountains offers a breathtaking ride along the "top" of the state. The Natural Bridge near Lexington, purchased by Thomas Jefferson in 1774 for twenty shillings, is one of the seven natural wonders of the world. Along the Virginia coast wild ponies are rounded up annually by saltwater cowboys. A visit to a Virginia vineyard is a reminder that this is where the American wine industry started. Historic battlefields throughout the state allow you to imagine the action of the Revolutionary and Civil Wars.

A trip to Virginia is a journey to the past. This is the heart of our country, where American heritage began.

Jamestown

Thirteen years before the Plymouth Pilgrims set foot on American land, three ships brought 104 Englishmen to establish a colony on the banks of the James River in Virginia. Named Jamestown after King James I, the seventeenth-century settlement is located in the Williamsburg area. You can witness the culture and history of Jamestown that have been brought back to life at the re-created Jamestown Settlement. Nearby, the site of the original Jamestown, run by the National Park Service, is open to the public.

In December 1606, three ships set sail for the New World from London. The *Susan Constant, Godspeed,* and *Discovery,* with 104 passengers, arrived April 26, 1607, at Cape Henry, now part of Virginia Beach. The new colony was financed by the Virginia Company, a joint-stock company founded by King James I.

The Virginia Company expected to profit from the great natural resources located in the New World. Its investors hoped to find a new passageway to the Orient and wanted to settle in this area before the Spanish, who were busy trying to establish colonies in America.

For two weeks the colonists searched for an easily defensible site to settle; they chose an area along the banks of the James River. They were not prepared for the grueling conditions they experienced in the years to come. Hot, humid summers, hostility from the Indians, and poor drinking

The reconstructed Jamestown Settlement, with "colonists" at work.
(Photo by Carrie Shook)

water nearly forced the colonists to abandon their hope for survival. Many settlers died from starvation and disease.

The colonists attempted several different industries, but all failed except for the cultivation of tobacco. The success of this crop provided the colony with economic stability.

Jamestown was the first successful and permanent English settlement in the United States. It served as the capital of Virginia until 1699, when the seat of government was moved to Williamsburg.

Jamestown is fascinating. Ruins of the original structure where the colonists manufactured glass, a museum containing seventeenth-century artifacts, and the original brick tower of the Jamestown Church, built in 1639, are must-sees. The outlines of the foundations of the colonists' homes and other buildings are also visible.

A mile up the James River is Jamestown Settlement, a living-history museum that re-creates life in early Jamestown. Self-guided tours lead you through replicas of a Powhatan Indian village and the fort constructed by Jamestown's first settlers. The village features reenactments of Powhatan life; costumed "interpreters" prepare meals, tan and cure animal hides, make tools from bones and antlers, weave baskets, and make pottery. Inside the fort are eighteen

Full-scale reproductions of the Godspeed, Discovery, *and* Susan Constant. (Courtesy Jamestown-Yorktown Foundation)

primitive wattle-and-daub structures (a woven framework of sticks covered with mud) with thatched roofs, representing Jamestown's earliest buildings. Men and women in period clothing perform militia drills, make tools, tend livestock and gardens, and prepare meals as their ancestors did in the seventeenth century. Here you are free to try your hand at gardening, cooking, and playing games. You can also participate in the militia musters conducted by men in military costume.

Other highlights of the park are re-creations of the original colonists' three ships. Visitors may board the *Susan Constant,* the largest of the three. An interpreter dressed in a costume representing clothing worn at the time of the voyage will tell you the story of the original voyage across the Atlantic. The reconstructed *Godspeed* successfully retraced the 1607 voyage from England, in 1985. The smallest ship, the *Discovery,* is often open to visitors and is used for demonstrations of sailing techniques.

Jamestown and Jamestown Settlement are American history re-created in living color. Jamestown Settlement is located at the intersection of Virginia Route 31 and the Colonial Parkway. Operating hours are 9:00 A.M. to 5:00 P.M. daily, except New Year's Day and Christmas, with extended hours during summer months. Call (804) 229-1607 for more information. There is a separate fee for the Jamestown National Historic Site. Call (804) 229-1733 for further information.

Yorktown

The last major battle of the Revolutionary War was fought at Yorktown in 1781. In the spring of that year, General Cornwallis of the British army led his troops into Virginia with orders to fortify a port in the Chesapeake Bay area, to use as a base for contact with the British fleet. Opposing the British was a small American force led by General Lafayette. Meanwhile, General George Washington had strategized that a combined land and naval battle coordinated with a French effort should occur in Virginia. Washington moved the bulk of the French and American forces south to Virginia, anticipating an opportunity to trap Cornwallis there.

On September 5, the French fleet defeated the British naval force, and a few weeks later Washington and the French general Rochambeau arrived at Yorktown and began their land siege. The British finally surrendered on October 19, 1781, in effect ending the Revolutionary War.

Several exhibits covering the Revolutionary period are open to the public at Yorktown. A walk through Yorktown is a walk through history. Main Street, which spans the town, has many restored eighteenth-century buildings, including the home of Governor Thomas Nelson, a signer of the Declaration of Independence.

At one end of the town is the state-operated Yorktown Victory Center, a museum that chronicles events of the American Revolution through multimedia displays, exhibits of art and artifacts, and living history. Exhibits include a collection of artifacts excavated from British ships sunk during the Siege of Yorktown. A twenty-eight-minute documentary film, "The Road to Yorktown," tells about events leading up to the siege. A Continental Army camp has also been re-created; men and women in Revolutionary-period costume prepare meals, perform drills, and engage in other everyday colonial activities.

The National Park Service administers the Yorktown Battlefield and Visitor Center, about two miles from the Victory

Yorktown Battlefield, where Lord Cornwallis surrendered to General George Washington on October 19, 1781.
(Courtesy Jamestown-Yorktown Foundation)

Center. The Visitor Center has a full-size replica of the quarterdeck of a British warship and a collection of Revolutionary War artifacts, including the field tents used by General Washington during the war. On the battlefield, reconstructed earthworks and siege lines mark the pattern of the British and American troops. The home of Augustine Moore, where surrender terms were negotiated in 1781, is on the battlefield tour.

Yorktown is where British rule ended and American independence began. You can almost hear the orders directed at soldiers by General Washington as he maneuvered his way through the British lines.

The Yorktown Victory Center is located on Virginia Route 238, just 12 miles from Williamsburg. It is open from 9:00 A.M. to 5:00 P.M. daily, year-round, except New Year's Day and Christmas, with extended hours in the summer. Call (804) 887-1776 for more information. The Yorktown Battlefield is also open to the public; entry is free. Call (804) 898-3400 for information.

Williamsburg

Where else could you trail behind a fife-and-drum corps on a Saturday afternoon or smell pungent black gunpowder from shots fired by a costumed militia company? Williamsburg, colonial capital of the United States, where history and heritage are frozen in time. Its 173 acres constitute one of the largest and most diversified museums in the world, with 90 acres of gardens maintained in original condition. Williamsburg is filled with reminders of the colonial era, and after sixty years of careful construction, 88 original buildings have been restored and more than 400 others have been reconstructed on historical foundations.

The site for Williamsburg was chosen by the Virginia Assembly; the settlement, originally called Middle Plantation, was renamed in honor of the reigning British monarch, King William III. In 1699 Williamsburg succeeded Jamestown as capital of Virginia. It remained the capital until 1780, when the state government was moved to Richmond.

Williamsburg was one of the most important ideological training grounds for American leaders. Not only did it serve as the capital of the Virginia colony for eighty-one years, but it was here that George Washington, Patrick Henry, George Wythe, Thomas Jefferson, and George Mason conducted their initial meetings to prepare the Declaration of Independence and the Declaration of Rights. And it was here that Patrick Henry delivered his famous "Caesar–Brutus" speech arguing against the British Stamp Act. Thomas Jefferson introduced his statute for religious freedom at Williamsburg, and the Virginia Constitution of 1776 was also born there.

The historical site extends a full mile, with an average width of half a mile. The same streets have been used since 1699, and they are normally closed to traffic so pedestrians are free to wander. Each year more than a million people visit the colonial capital to see the President's House at the college of William and Mary, the Wren Building, the 1770 courthouse, Bruton Parish Church, the Public Magazine, Market Square, and Wetherburn's Tavern. Restored homes include those that belonged to George Wythe, Peyton Randolph, John Brush and later Thomas Everard, James Geddy, and St. George Tucker.

A royal charter for a college in Williamsburg was granted on February 8, 1693, by King William III and Queen Mary II. This, the second college established in the country (after Harvard), was later named the College of William and Mary after its royal patrons; among its many notable alumni are George Washington, Thomas Jefferson, George Wythe, and Peyton Randolph. In 1695 the cornerstone was laid for the first building, then known simply as "The College." In the twentieth century the building was renamed the Wren Building after Sir Christopher Wren, who many believe was its designer. After surviving the damages of two wars and three fires, it was restored from 1928 to 1931. The Wren Building is the oldest academic building still in continuous use for instruction in the United States.

The President's House on the north side of campus has been the residence of every president of the college. Built in 1732, the house was used by Cornwallis as his headquarters and later by French officers after the Siege of Yorktown.

21

Excellent examples of successful reconstruction are the Governor's Palace, the capitol building, and the public hospital. Reconstruction is possible only after extensive archaeological, architectural, and historical research to determine the exact size, original appearance, and function of a building on its original site. Articles used in the reconstruction process include old deeds, wills, court records, insurance papers, inventories, letters, and books. Colonial methods of building and painting are also studied carefully.

The original Governor's Palace was completed in 1722 and became the new residence of Virginia's royal governor. It was considered one of the finest buildings in the country. When the majority of Virginians, even the well-to-do, lived in one-story houses composed of no more than two or three rooms, this home was really a palace! The elegant residence housed seven royal governors and the first two governors of the Commonwealth of Virginia, Patrick Henry and Thomas Jefferson.

On the night of December 22, 1781, a fire broke out in the palace; within three hours it was completely destroyed. All that remained of the central structure was a charred pile of bricks. The building became no more than a memory until the 1920s, when it was reconstructed to its original state.

The palace is surrounded by sixty-three acres of well-manicured gardens and lawns and a wonderful maze of thorn bushes that is as popular now as it was with colonial guests.

Nearly forty exhibitions are open to the public, including the restored 225 period rooms, each furnished with American and British antiques. There are over 100,000 examples of furniture, paintings, china, glass, pewter, textiles, tools, and carpets on display. Costumed "interpreters" provide background information about Williamsburg's history and culture, in the language spoken in colonial days.

In the twenty craft shops, costumed artisans demonstrate eighteenth-century tools in craftmaking of the period. Craftmakers include baker, basketmaker, blacksmith, bookbinder, bootmaker, cabinetmaker, cooper, instrument maker, jeweler and engraver, music teacher, printer, silversmith, spinner and weaver, wheelwright, and wigmaker. There is also an apothecary and a post office.

You can't visit Colonial Williamsburg without eating at one of the several historical taverns that line the streets. They are exact reproductions of eighteenth- and nineteenth-century taverns, built on original foundations. The reconstructed taverns serve many dishes that were popular with the colonists. During the evening hours, many of the taverns offer gambols, colonial games played hundreds of years ago.

The Raleigh Tavern, where the Phi Beta Kappa society was founded, is the most famous in town. Many patriots gathered here to voice their opposition to the policies of the British Crown and held important meetings that foreshadowed American independence. The tavern is now open for tours only, but the kitchen operates as a bakery serving colonial specialties including cookies, breads, and pastries that were once and still are popular.

The King's Arms Tavern was considered one of the most genteel eighteenth-century taverns and was patronized by a select clientele that included George Washington and Virginia's fourth governor, General Thomas Nelson, Jr. It too is open to the public and serves traditional southern dishes such as peanut soup, Virginia ham, game pie, and Sally Lunn bread (a British specialty).

Colonial Williamsburg represents the American struggle for independence. Important principles such as self-government, equality before the law, and religious freedom were established in Williamsburg by giant men in our na-

The Governor's Palace in Colonial Williamsburg was the official residence of the king's representative to the Virginia colony. Patrick Henry and Thomas Jefferson lived here as the first two governors of the commonwealth.

tion's history. They once walked these streets, and now you can do the same!

Begin your tour of Colonial Williamsburg at the visitors' center, where you can pick up an orientation map and tickets to the exhibits. Hours of operation are 9:00 A.M. to 5:00 P.M. daily. Call (800) HISTORY for more information and to make lodging reservations.

Those who want to re-create original colonial dishes on their own should be aware that in the past recipes had very sketchy instructions: "Add a little white wine," or "Add a piece of fresh butter," or "Place in an oven not too hot." Many ingredients called for in colonial recipes are no longer available or are not even considered edible, for example, ambergris, a waxy substance from the intestines of the sperm whale.

Chefs at Colonial Williamsburg have experimented with old popular recipes and have adapted them to the twentieth-century kitchen, without losing the flavor. The following recipes, among the most popular items ordered at the taverns, are very easy to prepare at home.

Raleigh Tavern Bake Shop's
Gingerbread Cookies

   1 cup sugar
   2 tsp. ginger
   1 tsp. nutmeg
   1 tsp. cinnamon
   $1/2$ tsp. salt
   $1 1/2$ tsp. baking soda
   1 cup margarine, melted
   $1/2$ cup evaporated milk
   1 cup unsulfured molasses

25

³/₄ tsp. vanilla extract (optional)

³/₄ tsp. lemon extract (optional)

4 cups stone-ground or unbleached flour, unsifted

Preheat oven to 375°.

    Combine the sugar, ginger, nutmeg, cinnamon, salt, and baking soda. Mix well. Add the melted margarine, evaporated milk, and molasses. Add the extracts if desired. Mix well. Add the flour 1 cup at a time, stirring constantly, until the dough is stiff enough to handle without sticking to fingers. Knead the dough for a smoother texture. Up to ¹/₂ cup flour may be added to prevent sticking, if necessary. When the dough is smooth, roll it out ¹/₄ inch thick on a floured surface and cut it into cookies. Bake on floured or greased cookie sheets in a 375° oven for 10 to 12 minutes. The cookies are done when they spring back when touched lightly. Makes 50–60 medium-sized cookies.

Raleigh Tavern Bake Shops
Sally Lunn Bread

1 cup milk

¹/₂ cup shortening

¹/₄ cup water

4 cups sifted all-purpose flour

¹/₃ cup sugar

2 tsp. salt

2 packages active dry yeast

3 eggs

Preheat oven to 350°.

    Lightly grease a 10-inch tube cake pan or a Bundt pan. Heat the milk, shortening, and water until very warm (about 120°). The shortening does not need to melt. Blend 1¹/₃ cups of flour with the sugar, salt, and dry yeast in a large mixing bowl. Blend the warm milk mixture into the flour mixture. Beat with an electric mixer at medium speed for about 2 minutes, scraping the sides of the bowl occasionally. Gradually add ²/₃ cup of flour and the eggs and beat at high speed for 2 minutes. Add the remaining flour and mix well at low speed. The batter will be thick but not stiff. Cover and let the dough rise in a warm, draft-free place (about 85°) until it doubles in size (about 1 hour and 15 minutes). Beat the dough down with a spatula or at the lowest speed on an electric mixer and place in the greased pan. Cover and let rise again in a warm, draft-free place until it has increased in bulk one-third to one-half (about 30 minutes). Bake in 350° oven for 40 to 50 minutes. Run a knife around the center and outer edges of the bread to remove it from the pan and place on a plate to cool. Sally Lunn bread is great for sandwiches!

King's Arm Tavern Cream of Peanut Soup

1 medium onion, chopped

2 ribs celery, chopped

¼ cup butter

3 tbsp. all-purpose flour

2 quarts chicken stock or canned chicken broth

2 cups smooth peanut butter

1³/₄ cups light cream

¼ cup peanuts, chopped (for garnish)

Sauté onion and celery in butter until soft but not brown. Stir in flour until well blended. Add chicken stock, stirring constantly, and bring to a boil. Remove from heat and puree in a food processor or blender. Add peanut butter and cream, stirring to blend thoroughly. Return to low heat but do not boil. Sprinkle with chopped peanuts and serve. Makes 10–12 servings. This soup is also good served ice cold.

King's Arms Tavern Corn Pudding

3 eggs

2 cups milk

½ cup light cream

1 1/2 tbsp. sugar

1/2 tsp. salt

2 cups corn cut from cob, or cream-style corn

1 cup bread crumbs

2 tbsp. butter, melted

Preheat oven to 350°.

Grease 1 1/2-quart casserole dish. Beat eggs until light and fluffy. Add milk, cream, sugar, and salt. Stir in corn, bread crumbs, and butter and place dish in pan of boiling water. Bake at 350° for 50 to 60 minutes or until custard is set.

The famous Raleigh Tavern of Colonial Williamsburg, where the Phi Beta Kappa society was founded. (Photo by Carrie Shook)

Fredericksburg

The history of Fredericksburg spans three centuries. George Washington grew up in the Fredericksburg area. His spirit lives on in almost all the town's historic attractions. The town is strategically located between two major capitals, Washington D.C., and the Confederate capital, Richmond, and its location was the source for several Civil War battles. The town is now full of historical homes, battlefields, and fabulous antique shops!

Washington spent some of his early years at Ferry Farm, across the Rappahannock River from Fredericksburg. It was here that Washington allegedly chopped down the cherry tree and told his father he could not tell a lie. The famous legend of Washington throwing a coin across the Potomac was an embellishment of a real event that took place in Fredericksburg (he actually threw a Spanish coin across the Rappahannock). Washington, who called Fredericksburg "the place of my growing infancy," left Ferry Farm in his early teens.

Washington continued to visit his mother, Mary Ball Washington, at Ferry Farm throughout his life. In 1772 he bought her a small white frame house in Fredericksburg, near his sister's house; his mother lived in this house for the last seventeen years of her life. The house is now open for tours and displays many eighteenth-century antiques that belonged to Mary Washington, including her "best dressing glass," which she willed to George. The house is located at 1200 Charles Street and is open daily from 9:00 A.M. to 5:00 P.M., with limited hours from November 1 to March 31. Call (703) 373-1776 for more information.

The Rising Sun Tavern belonged to Charles Washington, George's youngest brother. Built around 1760, it was Charles's home for over twenty years, and in 1792 was leased to John Frazier, who announced that he would open the house to the public as a tavern. Known first as the Eagle, then as the Golden Eagle, it was finally renamed the Rising Sun in 1821. The building has been completely restored and sections of the original bar have been assembled in the tap room. The bar, a structure with metal rods—as in a bank teller's station—is in the corner of the room. Patrons who drank were often rowdy, so it was not unusual for the tavernkeeper to serve from a locked enclosure; patrons could thus be kept from stealing money and liquor, as well. (This is how the word *bar* became associated with a drinking establishment.) The tavern is open for tours from 9:00 A.M. to 5:00 P.M. daily, except during winter months. Call (703) 373-1776 for more information.

The story of Kenmore, one of the most beautiful colonial mansions in the United States, begins in 1750 with the marriage of Colonel Fielding Lewis to Betty Washington, George's sister. Lewis began constructing a mansion and completed the house in 1775. Its ceilings have some of the finest decorative plasterwork in the country. The craftsman, who worked also at Mount Vernon, remains anonymous to this day. The garden, the size of a city block, is among the country's earliest horticultural restorations. Tea and gingerbread are served in the kitchen, a tradition started by the Washingtons. Visitors enter Kenmore through the Crowninshield Museum, which contains exhibits illustrating the history of Kenmore and the colonial period. Kenmore is open for tours from 9:00 A.M. to 5:00 P.M. daily, March through November. In December through February, hours are 10:00 A.M. to 4:00 P.M. daily. Call (703) 373-3381 for more information.

The law office of James Monroe is at 908 Charles Street. It was here that the famous politician first practiced law, from 1786 to 1789. Prominent among the many exhibits in the Law Office Museum and Memorial Library is a Louis XVI desk with secret compartments; on this desk, President Monroe signed the Monroe Doctrine and wrote his annual messages to Congress. Furniture Monroe purchased in France while he was minister to France (1794–1796) is also on display. Another highlight is the array of costumes worn by Monroe and his wife at the court of Napoleon and Mrs. Monroe's exquisite gems. The library contains thousands of books and historical manuscripts. The museum and library are open daily from 9:00 A.M. to 5:00 P.M. For further information, call (703) 373-8426.

Four major Civil War battles were fought in the Fredericksburg area, as the Union Army tried to gain control of the Confederate capital, Richmond. The battles of Fredericksburg, Chancellorsville, the Wilderness, and Spotsylvania Court House brought Robert E. Lee, Stonewall Jackson, Abraham Lincoln, Ulysses S. Grant, Clara Barton, Walt Whitman, and many others to the area. For two years the countryside in and around Fredericksburg was a bloody battlefield; combined Union and Confederate casualties in the four battles totaled over 100,000. In the winter of 1862, a simple stone wall on Fredericksburg's Sunken Road was the location of a clash that resulted in the death of 13,000 Union soldiers who struggled to capture the Confederate position above and behind the wall. The fighting continued nearby at battles of Chancellorsville (1863), the Wilderness (1864), and Spotsylvania Court House (1864). The National Cemetery contains the graves of over 15,000 Union soldiers and the Confederate Cemetery on Washington Avenue is the burial ground for over 2,000 mostly unknown Confederate soldiers. Among the known Confederate dead buried here are six generals and Lucy Ann Cox, one of the few women to be made an honorary Confederate veteran after bravely accompanying her soldier husband through four years of war. All battle-fields and cemeteries are open to the public. The National Park Service maintains the battlegrounds and has visitors' centers with maps and exhibits at both Fredericksburg and Chancellorsville.

Many things have remained unchanged since Fredericksburg was officially chartered in 1727. Today, several of the more than 350 eighteenth- and nineteenth-century buildings in the town's forty-block National Historic District are open to the public for tours. You can take a piece of Virginia's history home with you by visiting any of the ninety-six antique shops in the Historic District, all of which feature a wide variety of antiques and collectibles from the seventeenth century to today.

Begin your visit to Fredericksburg at the visitors' center at 706 Caroline Street, where you can pick up brochures and maps, see an orientation film, and learn of special events in the area. Call (703) 373-1776 for more information.

Lexington

Lexington (population 7,000) is a quaint town of beautiful eighteenth- and nineteenth-century houses in impeccable condition. Stonewall Jackson and Robert E. Lee lived here. Two schools in Lexington, Washington and Lee University and Virginia Military Institute, have very fascinating histories and museums.

Begin your tour of Lexington at the visitors' center, where you can pick up a walking-tour map and brochures, and watch an orientation slide show. Hours are from 9:00 A.M. to 5:00 P.M. daily, until 6:00 P.M. during summer months. Call (703) 463-3777 for more information.

Across the street from the visitors' center, horse-drawn carriages begin a tour of Lexington. For a small charge, the driver will take you on a thirty-five-minute drive through town, complete with a history lesson on the homes and buildings. The Lexington Carriage Company's hours are 9:30 A.M. to 5:30 P.M., Monday through Saturday. Call (703) 463-9500 for further information.

The Stonewall Jackson House, built in 1801, was occupied by Jackson when he was a professor of physics at Virginia Military Institute. Jackson lived here until he left to join the Civil War, from which he never returned. (For more on the house, located at 8 East Washington Street, see p. 61.)

Washington and Lee University (often called W&L) was founded in 1749, and is thus the sixth oldest institution of higher learning in the country. George Washington saved the college from financial ruin in 1796 by donating $50,000 of James River Canal Company stock to its endowment. General Robert E. Lee saved the school from post–Civil War obscurity by serving as its president from 1865 until his death in 1870. Less than six months after surrendering to the Union Army at Appomattox, Lee rode his horse, Traveller, to Washington and Lee and assumed the presidency. He established the School of Law there and the first journalism program in the country. The school remained all male until 1985.

The Lee House was built for Lee in 1869 while he was president of the university and has continued to serve as the home for university presidents since. The large porch around the home was built especially for Mrs. Lee, who was confined to a wheelchair. General Lee died in a room on the first floor of the house.

The Lee Chapel and Museum at W&L was built at Lee's request while he was president. The brick and limestone building, completed in 1868, was used for daily worship services by Lee and his students and remains an integral part of the university today. Lee moved his office to the lower level of the building, where it remains today, preserved much as he left it in 1870. The rest of the lower level became the Lee Museum in 1928. Many items belonging to the Lee family are on display, along with an extensive array of paintings, including the Washington-Custis-Lee Collection's portrait by Charles Wilson Peale of George Washington in the uniform of a colonel in General Braddock's British army. Lee, his wife, his father, and all but one of his children are buried in the family crypt. The remains of Lee's beloved horse, Traveller, are buried outside his office. There is no charge to visit the museum, which is open from 9:00 A.M. to 5:00 P.M., every day except Sunday, April through mid-

Robert E. Lee's tomb, in the Lee Chapel and Museum at Washington and Lee University. (Photo by Carrie Shook)

October (9:00 A.M. to 4:00 P.M. the rest of the year). Hours are 2:00 P.M. to 5:00 P.M. on Sundays. Call (703) 463-8768 for more information.

Virginia Military Institute became the nation's first state-supported military college, in 1839. The most famous professor at VMI, Stonewall Jackson, taught physics until he left to fight in the Civil War. Campus buildings such as the Barracks (begun in 1851), the Commandant's Quarters (1852), and the Superintendent's Quarters (1860) are highlights of a walking tour. Cadet guides are available at Lejeune for free guided tours of the post, at 11:00 A.M. and 3:00 P.M. on weekdays and 10:00 and 11:00 A.M. on Saturdays during the school year. In the summer months, they are available at 1:00 and 3:00 P.M. only. The George C. Marshall

Museum and Library offers a collection of memorabilia of VMI alumnus George Marshall, former Army chief of staff, secretary of state and defense, and winner of the Nobel Peace Prize. The VMI Museum contains hundreds of historical artifacts from the Revolutionary War to the twentieth century.

The theater at Lime Kiln offers outdoor performances in a unique setting during summer months. The theater is on the location of an old lime kiln built in the late nineteenth century. Here you can enjoy concerts, Shakespearean plays, and historical plays about Virginians. Professional actors and musicians of national and international acclaim are featured. Bring a picnic if you like. Call (703) 463-7088 for more information.

Virginia Homes

Many beautiful homes in Virginia have played an important role in the history of our country. Berkeley Plantation was the site of our country's first official Thanksgiving, even before the Pilgrims arrived at Plymouth Rock. Later the plantation was used as headquarters for the Union Army. During the Revolutionary War, Abram's Delight was a rest stop for many military leaders including Washington and Lafayette.

Washington's Mount Vernon, Jefferson's Monticello, Madison's Montpelier, and Monroe's Ash Lawn–Highland are cornerstones for learning about the presidents who lovingly built them. Robert E. Lee and Stonewall Jackson wrote much about their happy years spent as private citizens living in carefully built and decorated homes, which are open for you to visit and enjoy.

Every historical home in Virginia has an important story to tell. Touring the estates and viewing portraits and personal belongings will give you enormous insight into the true personalities of the great figures who once lived there.

Berkeley Plantation

The first Thanksgiving in America took place at Berkeley Plantation in Charles City, a small community along the historic James River, between Richmond and Williamsburg. History at Berkeley Plantation did not stop there, however: it was the home of William Henry Harrison, and it was there that the bugle call "Taps" was composed.

Charles City, settled originally in 1619, was formally called Berkeley Hundred. America's first official Thanksgiving was celebrated the same year, before the Pilgrims' landing at Plymouth Rock. Of course, Thanksgiving is an ancient custom long celebrated by many European and Asian nations to give thanks for a military victory or blessing. The better-known American Thanksgiving was celebrated by the Pilgrims after an abundant harvest in the fall of 1621: church services were held, and Pilgrims and Indians feasted together for three days. Although this Thanksgiving is more famous, it was not the first! A reenactment of the original American Thanksgiving takes place annually at Berkeley on the first Sunday of November.

Berkeley Plantation was the birthplace of Benjamin Harrison V, who signed the Declaration of Independence and served as governor of Virginia from 1781 to 1784. His son, William Henry Harrison, ninth president of the United States, was also born here. The property was originally purchased by the Harrison family in 1691, but it wasn't until

America's first Thanksgiving took place in 1619 at Berkeley Plantation in Charles City.

1726 that Benjamin IV built the present plantation house, a double-pile, two-story brick dwelling that is among the earliest of the great Georgian plantations.

Berkeley was pillaged by Benedict Arnold during his James River campaign in the Revolutionary War. Fortunately, the Harrison family was able to repair the damage and retain ownership until the mid–eighteenth century. During the summer of 1862, the plantation was occupied by the Union Army of the Potomac under the command of General George McClellan. It was then that "Taps" was composed by a soldier and sounded for the first time.

Berkeley Plantation is a wonderful place to visit around Thanksgiving. It is open to visitors daily, year-round. Call (804) 829-6018 for more information.

Abram's Delight

Abram's Delight, on a 583-acre plot of land, is the oldest house in Winchester County. In the 1730s, settler Abraham Hollingsworth first laid eyes on his land and declared it a "delight to behold." He built a small cabin, which his son Isaac replaced in 1754 with a two-story limestone house. The house has walls two and a half feet thick and was a grand mansion of its day. Its solid walls enabled it to withstand severe weather and Indian attacks. Abram's Delight entertained such notables as George Washington, the Marquis de Lafayette, Lord Fairfax, and General Daniel Morgan. A flaxseed-oil mill, a carding mill, and carding machines were later added to the property.

The house passed through five generations of Hollingsworths for nearly 200 years, until the last Hollingsworth, Miss Annie, left the house and moved to Winchester, where she died in 1930. Abram's Delight remained vacant until 1943, when it was taken over by the city of Winchester, which turned it over to the Winchester–Frederick County Historical Society, and it was opened as a public museum.

The museum, located at 1340 Pleasant Valley Road, is open from 9:00 A.M. to 5:00 P.M. daily, April through October. Call (703) 662-6519 for more information.

While you are in Winchester, visit Stonewall Jackson's headquarters and George Washington's Office Museum. Jackson's headquarters are preserved much as they were during his 1861–1862 stay, and they contain many Jackson heirlooms. Located at 415 North Braddock Street, the headquarters are open daily from 9:00 A.M. to 5:00 P.M., April through October. For more information, call (703) 667-3242. George Washington's office was used in 1755 and 1756, when he served as a commissioned officer in the Virginia Militia. It too is open daily from 9:00 A.M. to 5:00 P.M., April through October. Call (703) 662-4412 for further information.

George Washington's Birthplace

The Washington family's Popes Creek tobacco farm in Tidewater is the birthplace and boyhood home of our first president. This Westmoreland County national monument offers a memorial house, a working colonial farm, a weaving room, and a farm workshop.

Washington's father, Captain Augustine Washington, was a planter, active in the military and civic affairs of the colony. Between 1722 and 1726 he built the house in which George was born.

Like many farm families in the Tidewater community, the Washingtons raised tobacco on a modest plantation. Most plantations had slaves working the fields, tending the crops, carpentering, blacksmithing, coopering, spinning, and weaving. The rich tobacco leaves were harvested and cured, then boarded on merchant ships bound for England. In exchange for tobacco, planters ordered from English agents luxury items such as sugar, fine cloth, dinnerware, and wines, which could not be produced on the plantation. Farmers might wait up to a year for delivery.

George Washington was born on February 22, 1732. He spent his first three and a half years on the plantation. The family moved to Mount Vernon, and four years later they moved again, to Ferry Farm. George returned to the Popes Creek farm throughout his childhood, visiting relatives who lived there.

On Christmas Day, 1779, as General Washington was leading his Continental Army in the fight for independence, the Popes Creek tobacco farm mysteriously burned to the ground. The house was never rebuilt, but the foundations remain and five underground structures have been uncovered: the birth house, the smokehouse-dairy, the kitchen, and two unidentified rooms. Many archaeological searches have been conducted here since the late nineteenth century, and dozens of artifacts have been found, including eighteenth-century ceramics, jewelry, ornaments, glassware, smoking pipes, and hardware. The working plantation has been painstakingly reconstructed from these discoveries.

The weaving room offers demonstrations of period spinning and weaving. Discussions and demonstrations of the woodworking, blacksmithing, and leatherworking of colonial days are held in the eighteenth-century farm workshop. The memorial house, erected as a tribute to Washington, has rooms decorated in the style typical of eighteenth-

The memorial manor is a representation of the eighteenth-century plantation house where George Washington was born.
(National Park Service photo by Richard Frear)

The kitchen house at the Washington birthplace.
(National Park Service photo by Richard Frear)

century upper-class homes. The house was built of hand-made clay bricks and includes furniture believed to have been owned by the Washington family. Many other furnishings in the house are over 200 years old. The kitchen house was separate from the main house, as was common to lessen the danger of fire to the family. An eighteenth-century kitchen constructed on the original kitchen site is equipped with typical utensils of the day. The memorial house and the kitchen house were built and furnished in 1930–1931, and opened to the public in 1932, for the bicentennial of Washington's birth.

Today, the colonial vegetable and flower gardens are tended in the same manner as they once were by the Washington family. Livestock, poultry, and crops of the same varieties and breeds that thrived there in the eighteenth century are raised by traditional farming methods.

Throughout his adult life, President Washington often spoke of his boyhood memories of watching flowers bloom and growing vegetables in the garden. He saw himself first and foremost as a farmer, and once said, "No pursuit is more congenial with my nature and gratifications, than that of agriculture; nor none I so pant after as again to become a tiller of the earth."

Mount Vernon

America's most visited historic estate is Mount Vernon, home and final resting place of George and Martha Washington. Located in northern Virginia, the large plantation was owned by Washington's father, Augustine, until his death. The property and custody of young George were left to Lawrence, George's half-brother, who was fourteen years his senior.

The original house was a much smaller farmhouse built by Augustine Washington around 1735. George spent much of his youth after his father's death in this modest one-and-a-half-story home.

George had a great fondness for the estate. He visited the plantation several times each year while serving in the military and government, and he planned to spend his retirement there.

The large mansion you see today is the Mount Vernon built by George Washington. He found the original house too small and commissioned designs in 1773 for additions on the north and south ends. Over a period of almost twenty-five years, he personally supervised the evolution of Mount Vernon from a small farmhouse to a beautiful estate.

Washington chose a popular classical framework for his home, and construction of the two-and-a-half-story southern addition began in the summer of 1774. A study was built below the principal bedroom, and a simple back staircase connecting the two rooms allowed Washington to move freely and unnoticed between the two rooms. Work on the south wing was not yet complete when Washington left in 1775 for his seat in the Second Continental Congress. Despite a six-year absence from Mount Vernon, he kept a keen eye on improvements there; he monitored the workmen's progress through weekly correspondence with his cousin, Lund Washington, whom he left responsible for the project during the Revolutionary War.

In 1783 Washington returned to Mount Vernon and used his study to write letters offering his political vision and influence to James Madison, Alexander Hamilton, and other leaders. His stay was brief, however, as in 1789 he agreed to be the nation's first president. It wasn't until 1796, after two consecutive terms, that he was able finally to retire permanently to Mount Vernon.

In 1776 construction of a large two-story dining room began on the north addition; this took twelve years to complete. In 1781 the room was used by Washington and French generals to plan the Battle of Yorktown. The dining room is also where Washington received word he had been chosen the nation's first president and where, in 1799, his body lay in state for three days before burial.

Perhaps the most famous feature of Washington's home is the two-story outdoor living area that was used as a shady shelter during hot summers. Facing the Potomac, it was built in 1777 and is believed to have been designed by Washington himself.

Another highlight at Mount Vernon are the ornate ceilings created by the same stucco craftsman who worked on Kenmore, the house belonging to Washington's sister. The breathtaking ceiling, chimneypiece, and cornice in the dining room are all hand-carved. Many of the carved designs throughout the house have agricultural motifs, reflecting Washington's feeling that he was first and foremost a farmer.

The interior of the house is decorated with beautiful and

Mount Vernon, the plantation house and final resting place
of George Washington.

rare antiques. One of the most important pieces of furniture is the large bedstead on which Washington died. It is six feet, six inches long and was made to order in Philadelphia at Martha Washington's request. Another highlight is the mahogany harpsichord Washington ordered in 1793 for his step-granddaughter, Nelly, who was adopted (along with her brother, George Washington Parke Custis) by Washington after their father, Jacky, died. The finest piece of American furniture in the house is the mahogany tambour secretary in Washington's study.

Among the many treasures on display at Mount Vernon

are a flower-shaped diamond ring (six rose-cut diamonds clustered around a larger one) and a garnet necklace that belonged to Martha Washington. Her most prized pieces of jewelry were bracelets with glass miniatures in oval gold frames. When portrait artist Charles Wilson Peale went to Mount Vernon to paint a portrait of Washington in 1772, he also painted miniatures of Martha and her two children, Patsy and Jacky. A few years later, Peale added a miniature of Washington to Martha's collection.

Americans can find a piece of their own heritage in the home that belonged to the "Father of Our Country." Over thirty acres including lush formal gardens are open to the public on a daily basis all year long. Regular hours are 9:00 A.M. to 5:00 P.M. except during the winter season, when doors close at 4:00. Call (703) 780-2000 for more information.

Monticello

Thomas Jefferson's Monticello, "Little Mountain," is one of our country's foremost architectural masterpieces. At the age of fourteen, Jefferson inherited his father's 5,000-acre estate, which included four adjacent plantations in the Charlottesville area. Jefferson began construction of his own mountaintop estate in 1769, when he was twenty-six. He chose a neoclassical design after studying the works of sixteenth-century Italian architect Andrea Palladio. A perfectionist, Jefferson spent many years putting up and pulling down different structures until he found what he wanted. It wasn't until 1808 that Jefferson was satisfied and considered his house finished.

For over a quarter of a century, Jefferson served in numerous political roles. He was governor of Virginia (1779–1781), minister to the court of Louis XVI (1784–1789), first secretary of state (1790–1793), vice-president (1797–1801), and third president of the United States (1801–1809). Despite the demands of public office, he always found time to devote to architecture and garden design.

Few houses in the world reflect the personality of their owners quite as Monticello does. All aspects of its decor were overseen by Jefferson; his lifetime was spent collecting furniture and the other objects on display. Furniture was purchased from the foremost cabinetmakers in New York, Philadelphia, and Virginia, and a few pieces were crafted by his own staff at Monticello.

A view of Monticello's west front. (Photos of Monticello courtesy Thomas Jefferson Memorial Foundation, Inc./James Tkatch)

The eighteen-and-a-half-foot-high entrance hall, which Jefferson used as a museum, contains one of the largest private collections of natural history and Native American artifacts in the country. Jefferson commissioned the Lewis and Clark Expedition of 1804–1806 and requested they bring back souvenirs of the great West. A buffalo head, elk antlers, and a few mastodon bones that William Clark brought back for Jefferson from Big Bone Lick in Kentucky

51

Monticello, entrance hall: This room was referred to as the "museum" and contained eighteen pieces of statuary, animal bones, Indian antiquities, and curiosities from the Lewis and Clark Expedition. Several of these objects are currently on display.

are on display. Jefferson's seven-day clock in the hall not only tells time but also indicates the day of the week; hanging weights hit markers (Sunday, Monday, Tuesday, etc.) on the south wall. Unfortunately, the distance between markers was misjudged and no room was left for Saturday; holes had to be drilled in the floor to allow the weights to descend into the basement, where the marker for Saturday was placed.

There are many unique design elements in the house. The famous dome was the first built on an American house and is modeled after that of the ancient Temple of Vesta in Rome. Fourteen skylights were installed in various rooms—a very modern lighting technique, even by today's standards. Jefferson's strong interest in mechanics is seen in the variety of gadgets in his house: single-acting double doors, a revolving serving door with shelves, and a dumbwaiter on either side of a fireplace, each connected to the wine cellar below.

Monticello rests atop a beautiful mountain, with a view Jefferson described as "the Eden of the United States." The grounds are covered with magnificent ornamental and vegetable gardens, two orchards, a vineyard, and an eighteen-acre grove of trees. A believer in horticultural experimentation, Jefferson grew over 250 varieties of vegetables and herbs in his 1,000-foot-long garden. The English pea, his favorite vegetable, was crossbred in nineteen different varieties. Jefferson's detailed records have made it possible for workers to maintain the garden, orchards, and vineyards as they were originally.

Jefferson returned to Monticello in 1809 upon his well-earned retirement. He died in 1826 at the age of eighty-three and is buried in the family plot, which continues to be reserved for his descendants.

The restoration of the house and grounds, along with the continued acquisition of original furnishings, helps keep Monticello as it was when Thomas Jefferson roamed the halls. It is located 3 miles southeast of Charlottesville on Route 53. Monticello is open daily, except Christmas Day, from 8:00 A.M. to 5:00 P.M., and from 9:00 A.M. to 4:30 P.M., November 1 through February 28. Call (804) 295-2657 or 295-8181 for more information.

Montpelier

A beautiful 2,700-acre estate, Montpelier was first settled in 1723 by James Madison's paternal grandparents, and was passed down through three generations of Madisons. The home of the fourth president of the United States and his wife, Dolly, was built in 1765 and 1766.

Madison retired to Montpelier in 1817 and lived there for nearly twenty years. After he died, on June 28, 1836, he was buried there, and Dolly sold the estate including most of its furnishings and moved back to Washington, D.C.

The estate had changed hands six times between 1844 and 1901, when it was purchased by William duPont, Sr., who made vast alterations. He enlarged the mansion and built additional barns, greenhouses, staff houses, sawmill, blacksmith shop, dairy, and train station. Mrs. duPont created a two-and-a-half-acre formal garden. When their daughter, Marion, inherited the property, she added a steeplechase and initiated the annual Montpelier Hunt Races, still held during the first weekend of November. Upon her death in 1984, Montpelier was bequeathed to the National Trust for Historic Preservation.

After being used as a private residence for over two centuries, the estate is now open to visitors. In addition to the fifty-five-room mansion, there are more than 100 other buildings and landmarks, including stables, Madison's Temple, and his gravesite. There are extensive lawns and beautiful gardens.

Montpelier is 20 miles north of Charlottesville and 4 miles southwest of Orange on Route 20. It is open daily from 10:00 A.M. to 4:00 P.M., but hours vary during holidays. Call (703) 672-2728 for further information.

Ash Lawn–Highland

Ash Lawn–Highland was the home of James Monroe, fifth president of the United States (1817–1825), for over twenty-five years. His beloved "cabin-castle" was originally built in Albemarle County, on 1,000 acres he purchased for $1,000, adjacent to Thomas Jefferson's Monticello. Jefferson wished to form an intellectual and social community in the rural countryside surrounding Monticello and encouraged Monroe to live nearby.

Monroe planned to spend his retirement at the modest home he named Highland. Shortly after he purchased the estate, he was appointed American ambassador to France by President Washington. During his three-year absence, his uncle Joseph Jones, Jefferson, and James Madison began cultivating the Highland estate. Jefferson sent his gardener to plant an orchard; Madison sent potato seeds for the garden, bottled gooseberries, and dried cherries. The Monroe family moved into Highland in November 1799, and decorated the home very modestly, as they had returned from Europe heavily in debt. By 1825 Monroe's debts totaled over $75,000, and he was forced to sell Highland before he reached retirement.

Under one of the many owners who followed the Monroes, the house acquired the name Ash Lawn. In 1862 the house was purchased by Parson John Massey, who added a large wing and established a school to educate newly freed slaves of the area. In 1929 Jay Winston Johns bought Ash Lawn–Highland from Massey's descendants. Realizing the historical importance of the estate, Johns opened it to the public in 1931 and spent the remainder of his life acquiring Monroe memorabilia and appropriate furnishings. Johns died in 1974, leaving Ashlawn, its contents, and its remaining 535 acres to Monroe's alma mater, the College of William and Mary.

Ash Lawn–Highland and its furnishings reflect the aspects of Monroe's career that made him one of the most important presidents and civil servants in U.S. history. The estate includes antique French wallpaper, the family crib, and a bust of Napoleon presented by the emperor to Mon-

Peacocks roam freely at Ash Lawn–Highland.
(Photo by Carrie Shook)

roe. In the entrance hall are documents relating to the Monroe Doctrine of 1823, warning against European intervention in the Western Hemisphere. Also on display are portraits of the First Family and European royalty whom Monroe befriended during his terms as minister to France, to Britain, and to Spain. Now open to the public, Ash Lawn–Highland is an example of a typical early-nineteenth-century farm, complete with grazing cattle, sheep, and horses and carefully tended flower, vegetable, and herb gardens.

The original smokehouse still stands, but the slave quarters have been reconstructed. The grounds are surrounded by massive English and American boxwood hedges, and feature an ancient oak tree and several roaming peacocks. Their piercing screams served as protection in Monroe's day, and the birds continue to guard the estate today.

Eighteenth- and nineteenth-century activities such as wool carding, spinning, and open-hearth cooking are practiced at certain times of the year on the estate. One of the annual highlights is the Ash Lawn–Highland Summer Opera Festival (June through August), offering performances (in English) in a beautiful outdoor setting perfect for picnics. During Christmas, tours through the house are led by costumed guides who demonstrate traditional Christmas activities from Monroe's era and earlier.

Ash Lawn–Highland is open daily from 9:00 A.M. to 6:00 P.M., and 10:00 to 5:00, November through February. Ash Lawn–Highland is only a few miles from Monticello on Route 795. Call (804) 293-9539 for more information.

Stratford Hall Plantation

Another of America's great landmark houses is Stratford Hall Plantation, home of the Robert E. Lee family, in Stratford. Set high above the Potomac River, the 1,600-acre farm is among the oldest operating farms in the United States.

Few families in American history have produced as many members who served their country with distinction equaling that of the Lee family, four generations of whom lived at Stratford Hall. Thomas Lee was justice of Westmoreland, a member of the House of Burgesses, commander of the militia, a member of His Majesty's Council, and chief executive of Virginia colony. He was the father of five sons, all of whom became active in building the foundation of the United States. Richard Henry Lee made a motion for independence to the First Continental Congress, and both he and his brother, Francis Lightfoot Lee, signed the Declaration of Independence. Arthur and William Lee served as diplomats in Europe to recruit support for the American Revolution. In all, four Lees were members of the House of Burgesses and two were members of Congress. Robert Edward Lee, the last Lee born at Stratford Hall to live to maturity, became general and chief of the Confederate Army.

Thomas Lee completed building the plantation house in 1738. Its architectural style sets it apart from other homes of the same time period: it is an H-shaped house built entirely of local materials—trees were felled from a nearby forest, and bricks were made on site. The house is filled with antique furniture and oil portraits of the Lee family. One of the most beautiful and magnificent historical rooms in the country is the great hall, at the center of the house. This was the focus for entertainment on the plantation and was used primarily for dancing and receptions. A twenty-nine-foot-square room with a seventeen-foot-high tray ceiling, elaborately carved walls, and an exquisite chandelier, the great hall is decorated with American Chippendale furniture, English Eagle console tables, and a spinet and harp that were once played at colonial gatherings. High windows overlook the Potomac, meadows, and woods. A formal garden and a horse trail thick with wild flowers were Robert E. Lee's favorite spots.

The plantation operates today much as it did when the Lees owned it: corn, wheat, oats, and barley are ground by a water-wheel mill as they were 250 years ago. The mill operates on the second and fourth Monday of each month from 1:30 to 3:30 P.M. throughout the year and every Saturday afternoon during the summer. The Stratford Store sells products made at the farm.

The Stratford Dining Room serves a plantation lunch to visitors from April to November 1. The plantation is owned and operated by the Robert E. Lee Memorial Association, and is open for tours daily (except Christmas Day). Call (804) 493-8038 for more information.

The Stonewall Jackson House

The streets of Lexington are filled with beautiful historical homes, but the one at 8 East Washington Street is special. This landmark was once home to one of the most famous Confederate generals, Thomas Jonathan "Stonewall" Jackson, and his second wife, Anna.

At East Washington Street Jackson lived the normal life of a Lexingtonian and was very happy. The Jacksons bought the brick-and-stone town house for $3,000 in 1858 and moved in when Jackson was a professor of physics at Virginia Military Institute. While a resident of Lexington, he was a successful businessman and an active member of the community. A deacon in his church, Jackson founded and helped finance a Sunday school for the black population. His favorite pastime was tending the small vegetable garden behind his house. Jackson took his wife to New York City for several weeks each summer, where they spent their time visiting art galleries, touring, and purchasing furnishings for their new house.

On April 21, 1861, a courier arrived at the Jackson house with an urgent message ordering Jackson to take the VMI cadet corp to Richmond. He left the only home he had ever owned and was never able to return. Jackson, noted for his fierce determination, his sense of duty, his faith and deep devotion to God, rose rapidly from major to lieutenant general in the Confederate Army.

The restored kitchen in the Stonewall Jackson House in Lexington.
(Courtesy Stonewall Jackson House)

During the war years, Anna Jackson and their young daughter, Julia, moved to North Carolina to live with Anna's family. They did not return to Lexington until May 1863, to attend Stonewall's funeral. After the funeral, Anna stayed on to break up the household, and she never lived in the house again. For forty years it was left in the care of a local law firm, and used as rental property.

Many tenants lived in the house over the years, and it deteriorated badly. In 1906, the Mary Custis Lee Chapter of the United Daughters of the Confederacy purchased the house from Mrs. Jackson and transformed it into the Stonewall Jackson Memorial Hospital. For forty-seven years it was the only hospital in the county. As the hospital grew, the house underwent drastic changes, including the addition of a new façade, porches, wings, and partitions.

The house was sold in 1953 to the Stonewall Jackson

Memorial, Inc., in order to certify it as a national landmark. The organization removed the additions and began to collect the Jackson furnishings that once decorated the home, and the house opened to the public in 1954. The estate was turned over to the Historic Lexington Foundation in 1976, which began an extensive fund-raising effort to restore the home. The Foundation raised the necessary funds, and many outstanding Jackson belongings were purchased from all over the country.

All restoration decisions were based on exhaustive research, in order to return the home to its original condition. Everything from the furniture and floor coverings to the wallpaper and garden is authenticated from various sources, including a meticulous estate inventory made shortly after Jackson's death, a vast collection of his letters, and newspaper clippings.

The Stonewall Jackson House is open to the public from 9:00 A.M. to 5:00 P.M., Monday through Saturday, and from 1:00 to 5:00 P.M. on Sundays. Tours begin every half-hour. Call (703) 463-2552 for further information.

Oatlands

The Oatlands plantation, almost 200 years old, once encompassed over 3,000 acres and had a gristmill that supplied ground flour for local farms and residences (including President Monroe's nearby Oak Hill estate). The mill was so successful that a town, today called Oatlands Mill, grew around its outskirts.

The original owner of Oatlands was George Carter, great-grandson of Robert "King" Carter, nicknamed for his extraordinary wealth and influence. When King died in 1732, his estate included 330,000 acres of land; 1,000 slaves; 2,000 head of cattle; 100 horses; and nearly a third of the wealth in Virginia. In a lottery held for King's surviving children, George Carter received 5,000 acres in Fairfax and Loudoun counties, which included Oatlands.

In 1803 George Carter began constructing the Oatlands house, which took seven years to complete. Its bricks were molded and fired on the premises; the wood was brought from surrounding forests. The house is a three-story Georgian home typical of the early nineteenth century. In 1816, Carter built the gristmill that provided ground flour for Loudoun County farms. During the next few decades, alterations were made on the house: octagonal rooms and a portico with carved Corinthian columns was added, both reflecting the popularity of Greek Revival architecture. Carter completed the house in 1830 and lived there until his death in 1846.

Oatlands, a 200-year-old Virginia plantation, was the center of Washington, D.C., social life for many years. (Courtesy Oatlands)

His son, George Jr., tried desperately to maintain Oatlands through the hardships brought on by the Civil War. The house fared well through the war, escaping much of the damage other plantations suffered when Confederate troops stationed themselves there. George Jr. and his wife, Kate, worked hard to keep Oatlands, and were able to do so until 1897, when they were forced to sell the plantation to the Hutchins family, founders of *The Washington Post*. The Hutchinses never lived in the house; they boarded it up and sold it in 1903 to the William Corcoran Eustis family.

The Eustises completely repaired and restored the house and its grounds to their original splendor. Mrs. Eustis, daughter of Levi P. Morton, vice-president under Benjamin Harrison, acquired many antiques, which remain on display throughout the house. She expanded the formal garden with a reflecting pool, a bowling green, and a gazebo. A distinguished sportsman in Great Britain, William Eustis turned Oatlands into an English-style country manor, which became a focus for Washington social life: country weekend and garden parties attracted famous politicians and visiting European dignitaries.

The house, on its 261 acres, was donated to the National Trust for Historic Preservation by the Eustis family. Oatlands boasts one of the most beautiful gardens in the United States, with a reflecting pool, perennial garden, rose garden, bowling green, and over forty varieties of evergreens and hardwoods, both native and exotic.

Oatlands is located on U.S. 15, midway between U.S. 7 (Leesburg) and U.S. 50 (Gilbert's Corner) in Loudoun County. It is open from mid-March through late December. Hours are 10:00 A.M. to 5:00 P.M., Monday through Saturday, and 1:00 to 5:00 P.M. on Sunday. Call (703) 777-3174 for more information.

The White House of the Confederacy

The Museum of the Confederacy in Richmond houses the largest and most comprehensive collection of Confederate memorabilia in the world. The museum includes the "other" White House, which served as Confederate executive quarters during the Civil War. The mansion has a long and dramatic history and has been a private residence, the Confederate president's house, a military headquarters, and a school.

Built in 1818 by wealthy Richmond bank president Dr. John Brockenbrough, the house is located on the corner of Twelfth and Clay streets, in the fashionable Court End district. The two-story brick home features a large columned portico on its garden front and had several outbuildings, including a kitchen and servants' quarters.

In 1844 the Lewis Crenshaw family purchased the home, added a third story in the same design, and installed elaborate gaslights. The Crenshaws redecorated the house with the current style of wallpaper, carpets, draperies, and furniture. They remained there until the outbreak of war in spring 1861, when they fled Richmond.

When the capital of the Confederacy was moved from Montgomery, Alabama, to Richmond in May 1861, one of the Confederate government's tasks was to find a suitable

The White House of the Confederacy in Richmond.
(Courtesy Museum of the Confederacy,
Richmond/Katherine Wetzel Photography)

residence for the president and his family. The city of Richmond purchased the Crenshaw mansion for $42,800: $35,000 for the house and land, $7,800 for the furnishings.

President Jefferson Davis and his family moved into the house in early August 1861, and the mansion became the social and political center of wartime Richmond. Although many public events took place there, Davis and his wife, Varina, tried to maintain a normal life for their three children, Margaret, Jefferson Jr., and Joseph. Two more children, William and Varina Anne, were born in the house during the war. In contrast to his very formal public behavior, Davis was an affectionate father who often stopped important meetings to listen to his children say prayers. Tragically, his son Joseph fell from the railing of the south portico in April 1864 and died.

As spring of 1865 approached, the war situation became critical along the lines at Petersburg, Virginia, and President Davis was forced to send his family out of the city in late March. On April 2, General Robert E. Lee telegraphed that the city must be evacuated, so Davis and his staff also fled. The next day, the Union Army entered Richmond and received a formal surrender from Mayor Joseph Mayo. President Lincoln visited the Jefferson residence on April 4, and the Union officer responsible for taking and holding Richmond, General Godfrey Weitze, moved himself and his staff into the mansion, where they remained stationed for the next five years.

In 1870 Reconstruction ended in Virginia, and the federal government withdrew the last of its troops from Richmond, returning the mansion to the city. The city auctioned off its contents, and for the next two decades the mansion was used as a schoolhouse.

In 1889 the school board proposed replacing the dilapidated landmark with a newer facility. Fortunately, a group of prominent Richmond women organized to protect the mansion and acquired the property in 1894. After a complete restoration, the house opened as a museum to the public on February 22, 1896, the anniversary of Jefferson Davis's inauguration as president of the Confederacy.

The next eighty years were spent on a nationwide search to attract Confederate memorabilia for display in the museum. Many personal items belonging to the Davis family were donated to the museum, including original gaslights, draperies, wardrobes, beds, and paintings. A complete restoration was made possible by relying on old inventories listing the house's original contents, and on photographs taken of Union officers posing around the mansion after the 1865 occupation; the discovery of original wallpaper fragments was also crucial for the restoration.

The Museum of the Confederacy is located at 1201 East Clay Street in downtown Richmond, a short walk from the State Capitol. All exhibits in the museum are self-guided, and the White House is open by guided tour only on a first-come, first-served basis. Museum hours are Monday through Saturday, 10:00 A.M. to 5:00 P.M., and Sunday, 1:00 to 5:00 P.M. Tours of the White House are given during museum hours except on Mondays and Thursdays, when tours begin at 11:30 A.M. The last tour of the day begins at 4:00 P.M. Call (804) 649-1861 for more information.

Cyrus McCormick's Farm

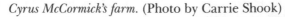

On this farm twenty-two-year-old Cyrus McCormick invented the horse-drawn mechanized reaper, which revolutionized American agricultural production. Completed in 1831, his invention helped farmers reap their grain with little manpower and encouraged American industry by producing cheaper food for factory workers. The 634-acre farm, with McCormick's workshop, a gristmill, and a house, is open from 8:30 A.M. to 5:00 P.M. daily; admission is free. The farm is located 20 miles north of Lexington on I-81 (exit 54). Call (703) 377-2255 for more information.

Cyrus McCormick's farm. (Photo by Carrie Shook)

Historic Garden Week

Each year, Historic Garden Week gives visitors a unique opportunity to see public and private homes. The homes are decorated with fresh flowers and beautiful gardens, and they are available for tour for one week each April.

The Garden Club of Virginia organizes the event and publishes a guidebook and several brochures. Regardless of weather conditions, homes and gardens are open in most towns, some for just one day, others for the entire week. You can drive through the state and visit a different town or city each day.

Historic Garden Week at the University of Virginia is a real treat. Founded in 1825 by Thomas Jefferson, the university has one of the most beautiful campuses in the country. Many of the buildings were designed by Jefferson, including the historic Lawn and Pavilion, and the Rotunda. Edgar Allan Poe lived in the Lawn rooms, which are still used today by seniors at the university. The Pavilion homes are occupied by faculty members and their families.

During Historic Garden Week, many Pavilion homes and several Lawn rooms are open for tours. This is the only opportunity visitors have to see the interior of the buildings. Gardens in the Pavilion contain rare plants of the Jeffersonian period.

A special highlight at the university is the evening candlelight tour of the Lawn given by student guides dressed in nineteenth-century costume. After dusk, the gardens are illuminated and the Lawn rooms are filled with candles.

Hundreds of beautiful private homes and nearly every important historical home—including the James River plantations, Monticello, Ash Lawn–Highland, and the Blue Bell Tavern of Williamsburg—participate in Historic Garden Week. This also is a good time to see rare antiques still belonging to private collections.

Festivities usually take place in late April and tickets are sold in blocks, or individually at each home. A free guidebook provides detailed information on the homes, gardens, and landmarks open during Historic Garden Week. To request a copy, send $1.00 with your name and address to: Historic Garden Week Headquarters, 12 East Franklin Street, Richmond, Virginia, 23219; you may also pick it up in person. Historic Garden Week Headquarters will also assist visitors in making lodging and touring arrangements. Call (804) 644-7776 or 643-7141 for information.

The Michie Tavern

The Michie Tavern's reputation as an "in" spot has been solid for over 200 years. Formerly a place for travelers to eat and spend the night, it now serves as a museum and restaurant.

In 1746 a Scotsman, John Michie, purchased land from Major John Henry, father of Patrick Henry. Michie's son, William, developed the land and opened a tavern on it in 1784. Travelers stopped at the tavern at its original location on an old stagecoach road in Earlysville, seventeen miles from the current location. The road was rocky, and sometimes no wider than a footpath. A ten-mile trip took up to a full day, and because taverns were scarce the Michie Tavern was a welcome place to spend the evening.

Typical meals included ham, bacon, dried venison, Indian bread, milk, and cheese. The tavern, which had a smokehouse, well, barn, and "necessary," served also as a local post office and makeshift school; its ballroom was sometimes used for Sunday worship.

During the eighteenth and nineteenth centuries, fees for room and board were not always paid in cash; payment by barter was customary. This was the American way—nearly two-thirds of all transactions were bartered: a pair of shoes from a shoemaker, furnishings from a cabinetmaker, or even a day of labor from a man without a particular trade were welcomed in lieu of cash.

A list of rules at the inn included: "No more than five to sleep in one bed." This might raise a few eyebrows today, but in the eighteenth century, strangers willingly shared beds. Guests were merely renting space to sleep, and since body heat worked to keep everybody warm in the poorly insulated buildings, folks didn't seem to mind bedding down with an unfamiliar fellow traveler. Those who refused to comply might be labeled unfriendly or unreasonably fastidious. During hot summers, travelers often slept outdoors.

Another rule at the inn was: "No boots to be worn in bed." Boots were expensive and were often stolen while travelers slept, so this was not a popular rule. Another was: "Organ grinders must sleep in the washhouse." Organ grinders, usually accompanied by monkeys, carried fleas, and were accordingly isolated from regular sleeping quarters. Local legend has it that William Michie required his servants to sing each time they brought meals to the dining area, to keep them from devouring the guests' food on the way. These sound like strange rules today, but then you don't see many organ grinders with small monkeys checking in at the lobby of your nearest motel!

At the turn of the twentieth century, a new highway replaced the stagecoach road and the tavern lost its popularity; its doors were eventually closed. In 1927 the tavern was carefully dismantled, and moved by horse and wagon to a site seventeen miles away. In the process, the old inn seemed to lose its roots, both literally and figuratively. It took nearly fifty years for the Michie Tavern to regain its rightful heritage and the credibility it has now. Charlottesville, a fourth of a mile from Monticello, has proved to be a more convenient location for the hordes of tourists who visit Jefferson's home.

The tavern is now a museum, which features guided tours through its rooms. Stop in to see one of the finest collections

Historic Michie Tavern first opened in 1784.
(Courtesy Michie Tavern)

of pre-Revolutionary American furniture and artifacts. The 200-year-old slave house has been converted into The Ordinary, a restaurant featuring typical colonial dishes and local wines.

The Michie Tavern is proud of the colonial cuisine served in the restaurant. The following recipes are among the most popular:

Stewed Tomatoes

4 cups whole tomatoes, peeled and quartered
1/2 cup sugar
1/4 stick (2 tbsp.) butter
1/2 tsp. salt
6 baked biscuits

Mix together tomatoes, sugar, butter, and salt. Crumble the biscuits and add them to the mixture. Cover and simmer in a saucepan over medium heat for 15 minutes. Makes 6 servings.

Colonial Fried Chicken

3/4 cup all-purpose flour
1 1/2 tbsp. oregano
1/2 tsp. paprika
1 tsp. garlic salt
1/4 tsp. pepper
1 2–3 lb. fryer, cut up
3 cups shortening

Combine flour and seasonings; roll the cut-up chicken in the flour mixture. In a Dutch oven or other heavy deep pan, fry chicken pieces in shortening at 350° for 12 to 15 minutes on each side, or until tender. Drain oil. Makes 4 to 6 servings.

Fruit Cobbler

3/4 cup sugar
2 tbsp. flour (if fruit is juicy)
1/8 tsp. salt
1/2 tsp. grated lemon peel
1 1/2 tsp. lemon juice

¹/₂ tsp. nutmeg

¹/₂ tsp. cinnamon

6–7 thinly sliced, pared, and cored cooking apples

1 package pie-crust mix (for 9″ pie)

1 tbsp. butter

Preheat oven to 425°.

Combine all ingredients except apples, pie crust, and butter. Place half the apples in a pie plate (line with pie crust first, if desired). Sprinkle with half the sugar mixture. Dot with butter. Add top crust, rolled to desired thickness. Dot crust with butter and make several slits to allow steam to escape. Bake 40 to 50 minutes or until filling is tender and crust nicely browned. Serves 10.

Historic Michie Tavern is just a fourth of a mile from Monticello on Route 53 in Charlottesville. Tours are offered seven days a week. The Ordinary is open for lunch from 11:30 A.M. to 3:00 P.M. Call (804) 977-1234 for more information.

Bed-and-Breakfast Inns

Imagine pulling into the driveway of a beautiful colonial home after a long day of driving and sightseeing, and walking through the door of a 200-year-old home filled with antiques. You place your bags in your room, and see a beautiful four-poster bed covered by a colorful antique quilt. Your window overlooks a quiet residential neighborhood with green rolling hills behind. In the morning, a delicious breakfast and an arrangement of fresh flowers on a long table await you in an elegant dining room.

A stay in a bed-and-breakfast is not only the most comfortable way to travel through the state, it is the best way to experience the true personality of Virginia. When you choose to stay in a historical home, you may select a place where famous Americans such as Thomas Jefferson or George Washington stayed when they traveled to that area. B&Bs are especially fun for the lone traveler, as they are a warm, friendly alternative to noisy impersonal motels.

When you are in Lexington, try to stay at one of three historic country inns: the McCampbell Inn, the Alexander-Withrow House, or Maple Hall. The first two are across the street from each other on Main Street in downtown Lexington. Maple Hall is six miles north, off I-81 at exit 53. The in-town inns are fully restored and offer a variety of rooms with private baths, wet bars, and antique furnishings. The McCampbell Inn, built in 1809 by John McCampbell, fea-

79

tures numerous verandas with rocking chairs and private entrances. One of Lexington's oldest and most elegant buildings, the six-suite Alexander-Withrow Inn, was built in 1789 by William Alexander. Maple Hall was constructed by John Beard Gibson around 1850 on the 257-acre Maple Hill Plantation. The lovely brick home, graced by towering white columns and a beautiful interior laden with antiques, offers a variety of outdoor activities. Bird lovers, wild-flower seekers, and explorers will have a wonderful time walking the several miles of paths on the property. There are also a tennis court, a swimming pool, and a fully stocked fish pond for the avid fisherman. For reservations at any of the three inns, call (703) 463-2044.

An additional special feature of Maple Hall is its elegant dining room, which serves Virginia specialties. The most popular dish is Stuffed Pork Chops Louise, named for Mary Louise Viar Rhodenizer, a lifetime resident of Rockbridge County, Virginia.

Stuffed Pork Chops Louise

   $\frac{1}{2}$ cup apple cider

   $\frac{1}{2}$ cup honey

   2 tsp. cinnamon

   2 tsp. ground ginger

   2 tsp. dry mustard

   1 tbsp. cornstarch

   1 cup raisins

   3 cups diced canned pineapple

   3 oranges, sectioned, with seeds and white membranes removed

   10–12 pork chops (about 6 oz. each), pocketed

   Preheat oven to 450°.

For the stuffing, mix apple cider, honey, spices, cornstarch, and fruit in a sauté pan; heat for a few minutes, until thickened. Remove from heat. Sauté the chops over medium heat for about 2 minutes on each side. Put 2 tablespoons of stuffing in the pocket of each chop. Bake at 450° for 10 to 15 minutes or until done. Serves 5 to 6 people (2 chops per serving.)

While driving down Skyline Drive, a great place to stop for a night's rest is the Jordan Hollow Farm Inn in Stanley, on the rolling meadows at the foot of the Blue Ridge Mountains. The inn is surrounded by a 200-year-old horse farm, and guests are welcome to take horse rides on trails that stretch into the mountains. The inn, also two centuries old, is a colonial farmhouse that has sixteen rooms with private baths, a library, a swimming pool, and four charming dining rooms offering country cuisine. Jordan Hollow Farm Inn is located about 15 miles south of Luray and is open all year. Take Route 340 south toward Stanley, turn left on 624, left on 689, and right on 626. Call (703) 778-2209 for reservations.

Another good overnight stop near Skyline Drive is the Inn at Narrow Passage in Woodstock. Overlooking the Shenandoah River, this log inn has been a stopover for travelers since the early 1740s. Several Indian raids took place near the site, and Stonewall Jackson headquartered here when the Confederate Army clashed with Union soldiers in the Shenandoah Valley. Narrow Passage has been restored to its eighteenth-century appearance, with original fireplaces in working order, gleaming pine floors, and exposed log walls. The twelve guest rooms are decorated with antiques, and most have wood-burning fireplaces. A hearty fireside breakfast is served in the paneled dining room. The inn is located 3 miles south of Woodstock on U.S. 11, off I-81 at exit 72. Call (703) 459-8000 for reservations.

Charlottesville offers a unique experience with true southern hospitality. Guest Houses Bed and Breakfast, Inc., arranges reservations in private homes and cottages in the Charlottesville area. Comfortable rooms and continental breakfasts await you in local homes where you are a family's guest, or you can rent your own home or cottage. Several price ranges are available. For the best selection, call several weeks before you travel. For reservations, call (804) 979-8327 during office hours, 1:00 to 5:00 P.M., Monday through Friday.

The Richard Johnston Inn in Fredericksburg is conveniently located in the historic Old Town. Built in 1789, the inn offers a sitting room, a library, an elegant dining room, and a variety of suites and bedrooms furnished with early American and English antiques. Every antique bed is covered with a handmade Amish quilt, and several rooms have working fireplaces. A breakfast of fresh fruit, homemade Danishes, coffee, tea, and juice is served on a long formal dining table decorated with fresh flowers. The inn, at 711 Caroline Street, is open all year. Call (703) 899-7606 for reservations.

The above are just a few suggestions of good homey places to stay; there are of course hundreds of others located throughout the state. Consult a country inn guide for more listings.

Appomattox Courthouse

Appomattox Courthouse, a small town east of Lynchburg, is where the United States really began. Here, in the McLean home, the Confederate Army of Northern Virginia, headed by General Robert E. Lee, surrendered to the Union Army of the Potomac, headed by General Ulysses S. Grant.

General Grant ended the war by exhausting the southern

Appomattox Courthouse National Historical Park, where General Robert E. Lee surrendered to General Ulysses S. Grant in 1865.

armies in a final struggle at Petersburg. After the defeat, Lee drove his dwindling army west and found himself surrounded by Grant's troops as his men approached Appomattox Courthouse. There, on April 9, 1865, Lee surrendered what was left of his army to Grant.

Grant gave Lee generous surrender terms. He agreed to feed starving Confederate forces from Union supplies and allowed Confederate soldiers to keep the horses they owned already (this was important because horses were needed for plowing southern farms). Instead of sending southern soldiers to prisoner-of-war camps, Grant let them return home after they swore an oath never to fight the Union Army again. Grant further promised Lee and other southern leaders that they would not be arrested or punished for treason.

Appomattox Courthouse has been preserved as it was during the nineteenth century, and The McLean House is open for tours daily. The town is located off U.S. 460 approximately 30 miles east of Lynchburg. Call (804) 352-8987 for more information.

Arlington National Cemetery

One of the most historically significant cemeteries in the world, Arlington National Cemetery, is the resting ground for thousands of American soldiers. It is located along the Virginia bank of the Potomac River, directly across from Washington, D.C.

The land originally belonged to Martha Washington's grandson, George Washington Parke Custis, who was adopted by her husband. As a memorial to Washington, Custis erected a mansion on the grounds to house the many relics he had acquired from Mount Vernon. Custis's daughter, Mary Anne Randolph Custis (General Robert E. Lee's wife) inherited the Arlington estate, and the house became known as the Lee Mansion. It became part of Arlington National Cemetery in 1864, and the name Lee Mansion was used until 1955, when it was officially changed by Congress to Custis-Lee Mansion.

During the Civil War, northern troops seized Arlington and used the grounds for camping and the house as their headquarters. The first soldier to be buried in the cemetery was a young unknown Confederate soldier who died in battle. Stretching for over a quarter of a mile are graves of approximately 3,800 former slaves, innocent victims of the War Between the States. Enslaved men, women, and children were buried in 1864, 1865, and 1866 in the oldest part of the cemetery, near the Ord-Weitzel Gate.

Arlington National Cemetery.

In 1864 Arlington became a national military cemetery. Rolling lawns, majestic trees, and beautiful flower beds fill the 408 acres. An impressive display is "The Fields of the Dead," which consists of long rows of plain white headstones of thousands of soldiers who died for their country. The Eternal Flame is a tribute to the memory of President John F. Kennedy, who is buried at Arlington. William Howard Taft, Robert Todd Lincoln, William Jennings Bryan, George Westinghouse, Admiral Robert Peary, and General John J. Pershing are among those honored by monuments at Arlington.

The Battle of Bull Run is commemorated by a granite tomb that holds the remains of 2,000 unidentified soldiers. Another memorial is dedicated to those who gave their lives for their country in the Spanish-American War. In 1921 the body of an unknown soldier killed in World War I was brought to lie beneath a tomb inscribed: "Here Rests in Honored Glory an American Soldier Known but to God." Thirty-seven years later, bodies of unknown soldiers who died in World War II and the Korean War were interred next to the World War I tomb, and Congressional Medals of Honor were placed on their graves. A simple military service is conducted each year on Veterans Day and an honor guard is always at the tomb.

The Museum of American Frontier Culture

The Shenandoah Valley was one of the first frontier regions in America to be settled by the early colonists. The Museum of American Frontier Culture in Staunton maintains national and international awareness of the important contributions made by the settlers in America's first western frontier. The museum, founded in celebration of America's bicentennial, is unique in its presentation of outdoor, living history.

The museum accurately reconstructs four different working farmstead environments. Three are similar to the European farms that settlers would have left behind in England, Ireland, and Germany. The fourth is American and reflects the melding of many European influences among early immigrants. All four farms raise the livestock and crops typical to each country represented. Trained staff, dressed in farmer's clothes of the period and region, sow, reap, and plow the fields; milk the cows; feed the livestock; spin, weave; and cook just as the real farmers. You are free to watch the food preparation in the farm kitchens, and to taste the results, such as Dutch apple pie baked over hot coals in the fireplace.

The German farm features a late-seventeenth-century house that was brought to Virginia from Hordt, in the

Rhineland-Palatinate region. The farmhouse has a timber frame and a clay tile roof. The main barn is made of timber with wattle-and-daub infill, and the tobacco barn is primarily wood. This farm is typical of those in the Rhineland-Palatinate, and it grows typical German crops such as rye, wheat, oats, tobacco, grapes, cabbage, and sugar beets.

The English farm is replicated from the early-seventeenth-century Northchapel Parish community, near Petworth, West Sussex. The farm consists of two timber-framed barns with grain storage, a threshing area, and a cart shed. There are a lime kiln, an apiary, and an apple orchard on the farm. Crops such as wheat, oats, barley, and peas are harvested from the fields, and cattle, draft horses, sheep, pigs, oxen, and other livestock are raised on the farm.

The early-nineteenth-century Scotch-Irish farm comes from Drumquin, a town in County Tyrone, Northern Ireland. The farm buildings have two-to-three-foot-thick stone walls and roofs thatched in the traditional Scotch-Irish manner. The main structure is a two-room sandstone cottage with an attached barn. Another barn has a pig sty and a chicken house nearby. Pigs, cattle, horses, and chickens live on the farm.

The American farm, representing pre–Civil War Virginia, was originally located in Eagle Rock, Botetourt County. The relocated log house is two stories high and has an adjacent one-story log kitchen. The farm has a double-pen log barn and single-pen log tobacco barn, stone springhouse, smokehouse, buggy shed, bee house, produce house, washhouse, chicken house, lime storage shed, and corn crib.

The "living farms" lie along the Warrior Path, a trail used by Indians who traveled through the Shenandoah Valley. The seventy-eight-acre outdoor museum site includes what was once part of the Great Philadelphia Wagon Road used by European settlers to travel to the Appalachian frontier.

American farm from the pre–Civil War period, at the Museum of American Frontier Culture.
(Courtesy Museum of American Frontier Culture)

Annual events at the Museum of American Frontier Culture include the Spring Planting Festival in mid-April; the Frontier Festival in September, with crafts, food, and entertainment of the 1700s and 1800s; the Harvest Home and Halloween Celebration in October, with harvest festivities, ghostly pranks, and games of the 1800s; and a traditional Christmas on each farm as celebrated long ago in England, Germany, Ireland, and America. Winter workshops, held in January and February, offer educational programs that focus on traditional cooking, crafts, and threshing. A visit to the museum is a step into the past. Here one can witness a living representation of early America.

The museum is located at the intersection of I-81 and I-64 in Staunton. Take I-81, exit 57, to Route 250 West. At the second stoplight, turn left onto Frontier Drive (Route 644). The museum is open daily from 9:00 A.M. to 5:00 P.M., and until 8:00 P.M. between Memorial Day and Labor Day. The museum is closed on Christmas and New Year's Day. Call (703) 332-7850 for more information.

Natural Bridge

Natural Bridge is beautiful, and a bargain as well! Thomas Jefferson knew a good deal when he saw one, and quickly fell in love with Natural Bridge, one of the seven natural wonders of the world. For the "sum of twenty shillings of good and lawful money," he purchased the bridge and its 157 surrounding acres from King George III of England. By today's exchange, this cost him less than five dollars.

While president, Jefferson built a modest log cabin and surveyed the property, making what is believed to be the first map of the area. He predicted that the bridge would be a "famous place that will draw the attention of the world" and invited many notable friends to visit it: Henry Clay, John Marshall, and James Monroe were among the frequent guests at his cabin. Other visitors included Davy Crockett, Daniel Boone, Sam Houston, and Andrew Jackson. George Washington surveyed the bridge and surrounding area in 1750, having been commissioned by Lord Halifax, the proprietor of the Northern Neck of Virginia. While there, Washington carved his initials on the southeast wall of the bridge; they are still visible, thirty-three feet above Cedar Creek.

The bridge joins two mountains and for centuries stood as a vital natural crossing over Cedar Creek for the Indians of the area. It is still used for transportation, as U.S. Route 11.

Millions of years old, Natural Bridge was once part of the

Natural Bridge was once owned by Thomas Jefferson.
(Courtesy Natural Bridge Village)

roof of an immense cave. The imposing limestone monument is 215 feet high, 90 feet long, and varies from 50 to 150 feet in width. It can be approached from the edge of a canyon by a walkway beside the creek, and is flanked by a series of beautiful waterfalls and trees over 1,000 years old.

"The Drama of Creation," a spellbinding forty-five-minute musical interpretation of the seven days of creation, is performed here nightly (twice nightly during the summer). Features of the bridge are illuminated, with narration accompanied by an organ and chorus.

Natural Bridge is located off I-81 south of Lexington. For more information, call (800) 533-1410 in Virginia, or (800) 336-5727 outside the state.

Virginia Caverns

The caverns of the Shenandoah Valley once served as ancient Indian burial grounds and later as a hospice for American soldiers during the Revolution. There are of course many caverns in the valley, but the grandest are the magical Endless and Luray Caverns.

Endless Caverns in New Market were discovered by two boys in October 1879. When their dog chased a rabbit up a hill and it disappeared under a rock, the curious youngsters lifted the rock and were astonished to find a deep tunnel. They explored the hole and were amazed to discover an underground world with winding channels and many large rooms. Because, even after years of exploration, no one found an end to any of the halls; the caverns were named Endless.

During the early years, tours were conducted by candlelight. Now the caverns are equipped with modern lighting that dramatically highlights the natural beauty of the stalagmites and stalactites. The caverns were officially opened to the public in 1920 and were completely renovated after an intensive two-year effort by the current owners, the Berdeaux family. Over $1 million was invested before the caverns reopened in 1986.

Highlights at Endless Caverns are Snow Drift, Diamond Lake, the Underground Cathedral, and the Palace of the Faeries. Each glittering room has a variety of stalactites,

The only "stalacpipe" organ in the world is at Luray Caverns.
(Courtesy Luray Caverns)

stalagmites, giant columns, shields, and flowstone and lime-stone pendants. Tours are offered year-round, seven days a week, and a comfortable fifty-six degrees is maintained at all times. Tours begin at 9:00 A.M., and closing times vary throughout the year. To get to Endless Caverns, take I-81 to exit 66. Go north on U.S. 11 for 3 miles to the cavern entrance. Call (703) 896-CAVE for more information.

The caverns of Luray, a few miles from Endless Caverns, were discovered in August 1878 by two explorers, Andrew Campbell and Benton Stebbins. They lowered themselves into winding passageways, which extended from one large room to the next. Since their spectacular discovery, millions of visitors have toured Luray Caverns to see the crystal-clear pools, colorful walls, and fantastic formations.

The greatest attraction is the world's only "stalacpipe" organ. In 1954 Leland W. Sprinkle took his young son to the caverns for the boy's fifth birthday. Sprinkle, an electronics engineer and accomplished organist, was intrigued by the clear tone made when a guide tapped a stalactite. He designed an organ that uses the beautiful formations. When the stalactites are tapped by rubber-tipped plungers, the sounds are concert-quality pitch. The Great Stalacpipe Organ is played from a large console operated by the organist. When standing in the center of the "cathedral" and listening to special arrangements, many agree that man's genius and the hand of God are in perfect harmony.

Luray Caverns are open every day of the year. The caverns open at 9:00 A.M.; closing time varies during the year. Take I-81 to exit 67, and go east on U.S. 211 for 13 miles to Luray. Call (703) 743-6551 for additional information.

The caverns of the Shenandoah Valley are great places to visit under any weather condition, all the year round.

Skyline Drive

The 105-mile drive across breathtaking Shenandoah National Park, is famous Skyline Drive. Wildlife—from black
bears, deer, and bobcats, to over 200 species of birds—is
found in the lush forest park. Seventeen kinds of wild or-
chids dot the miles of trails, and cool waterfalls and excellent
camping and picnic grounds await the weary traveler.

There are several places to stop and enjoy the view along
the drive, including Skyland Lodge, Big Meadows Lodge,
and Lewis Mountain. Skyland Lodge, at the highest point on
the drive, was founded in 1894 and offers rustic cottages,
live entertainment, horseback riding, and park naturalist
programs. Various special events are planned throughout
the summer at Skyland: Mountain Heritage Festival Days,
for example, features special dancing groups, dulcimer-
making demonstrations, and much more. Skyland's season
is from late March through December. Call (703) 999-2211
for reservations. The large, rustic Big Meadows Lodge, at
Milepost 51 on Skyline Drive, serves Virginia specialties in
its dining room and offers entertaining, informative camp-
fire programs. Big Meadows Lodge is open mid-May
through October. For information and reservations, call
(703) 999-2221. Lewis Mountain features economical furnished cottages with fireplaces and picnic tables. Call (703)
999-2255 for more information and reservations.

Family campgrounds are at Mathews Arm (mile 22.2), Big

Meadows (mile 51), Lewis Mountain (mile 57.6), and Loft Mountain (mile 79.5). Hookups for electricity, sewage, and water are not provided. For campground information, call (703) 999-2266. A free camping permit, required for all back-country camping, can be obtained at entrance stations, visitors' centers, and park headquarters, or by mail.

Skyline Drive is easily accessible from Interstates 64, 66, and 81. The north-south drive is between I-66 and I-64 and parallels I-81. While on the drive, it is convenient to stop in New Market and Luray to see Endless and Luray Caverns and the New Market Battleground. There are a number of bed-and-breakfast inns in the area.

Wild Ponies

The wild ponies of Assateague Island appeared mysteriously—how they got there is anyone's guess! One theory is
that as far back as the seventeenth century, ponies aboard a
shipwrecked Spanish galleon swam ashore and fed on grass
and seaweed on the island. Another, more likely theory is
that the ponies descended from domestic horses that once
grazed in the area. In the 1600s, mainland farmers' crops
were damaged by free-roaming livestock and they de-
manded some restrictions be placed on the animals. A law
passed by the colonial legislature required fencing and
heavy taxation for all domestic animals. Local residents
chose to use parts of Assateague as a corral for livestock and
horses. The island was an economical setting for keeping the
animals.

Approximately 300 wild ponies inhabit Assateague, con-
tent to feed on salty cord grass, beach grass, thorny green-
brier stems, bayberry twigs, rose hips, seaweed, and even
poison ivy.

Like most wild animals, these ponies form herds with a
single stallion accompanied by many mates and offspring.
When young stallions reach maturity, the dominating stallion in the herd forces them out, and they must fend for
themselves. A stallion governs his herd through various
body postures and verbal signs.

New Orleans has the Mardi Gras, New York has the Macy's

Thanksgiving Day Parade, and Chincoteague has its annual Pony Penning Day, an internationally known event that originated on the island approximately 300 years ago. On certain festival days in the seventeenth century, wild ponies were captured and then chosen by colonists. Modern Pony Penning Day began in 1924 in an effort to raise funds for the Chincoteague Volunteer Fire Department. A herd, rounded up by local cowboys, swims across the narrow channel from Assateague Island to the carnival grounds at Chincoteague Island. The majority of foals and yearlings are auctioned off and the remaining ponies are taken back to Assateague. The auction helps prevent overpopulation; the island has only enough vegetation to support a limited num-

A herd of wild ponies swim from Assateague Island to Chincoteague Island, home of the annual Pony Penning Day.
(Photos Courtesy Chincoteague Chamber of Commerce)

Wild ponies grazing on Assateague Island.

ber of ponies. The average bid for a pony is $225. The wild foals are easily tamed and trained.

Pony Penning Day has become more than just a fund-raiser; it is now a great homecoming for all past and present residents of the Chincoteague area. As many as 40,000 people are attracted to Chincoteague for the festivities, which include a delicious dinner and wild-pony rides.

The ponies of Chincoteague were made famous by Marguerite Henry, an author of children's books. Her *Misty of Chincoteague* (later a film) made the island a major tourist attraction. Misty was a real wild pony that Henry purchased and took back to her home in Illinois. Misty was taken back to Chincoteague a few times to be bred with a wild stallion, and she had three foals. Stormy, the youngest, still lives on the island. Misty died at age twenty-six in 1972, but her legend lives on in Marguerite Henry's stories.

Barter Theatre

Forget Broadway's incredibly long lines and exorbitant ticket prices. Go to the Barter Theatre, also known as the "State Theatre of Virginia," America's longest-running professional resident theater. This world-famous organization is nestled in the highlands of southwest Virginia, in a quaint town called Abingdon. The nation's first state theater was started here during the Depression by an aspiring young actor, Robert Porterfield.

During the first few seasons, the members of the company lived in empty buildings of local Martha Washington College and produced their work in the town hall across the street. There wasn't much money for entertainment, so playwrights such as Austin Strong, Robert Sherwood, and Thornton Wilder agreed to accept hams and other food items as payment.

The theater has hosted top names in show business. Many alumni have continued their successful careers on stage, television, and the silver screen: Margaret Wycherley, Gregory Peck, Hume Cronyn, Frank Lovejoy, Henry Fonda, Ethel Barrymore, Patricia Neal, Ernest Borgnine, Ned Beatty, Claude Akins, Gary Collins, David Birney, among others.

Professional productions, which run from April through October, range in style and period, and feature both new and celebrated actors. The theater is nonprofit and serves as an educational and cultural experiment, offering workshops

The internationally known Barter Theatre of Abingdon.
(Courtesy Barter Theatre)

and internships to aspiring actors. The unknown you see onstage might be next year's Robert Redford!

Over fifty percent of the Barter's patrons are visitors from outside the United States. The theater is located off I-81 at exit 8, at the intersection of U.S. Highways 11, 19, and 58. For information about performances, call the box office at (703) 628-3991.

While you are in Abingdon, eat at The Tavern, 222 East Main Street. The restaurant is in the oldest building in the area, dating from 1779, which was a tavern and overnight inn for stagecoach travelers. Andrew Jackson, King Louis-Philippe of France, and Henry Clay, to name a few, stayed here. Call (703) 628-1118 for reservations.

The Norwegian Lady

Virginia Beach is home to a beautiful Norwegian lady who spends all of her time guarding the rolling sea. She is a statue commemorating the wreck of the *Diktator*, which sank about 300 yards offshore. During the last few hundred years, there have been dozens of shipwrecks along the Virginia coast, but the wreck of the *Diktator*, on March 27, 1891, was one of the worst.

The three-masted ship had originated in Pensacola and was bound for Hartlepool, England, carrying a cargo of yellow pine timber, when strong winds off the Florida coast caused minor damage. The storm became more severe, and as the 114-ton ship headed toward the Virginia coast for repairs, it was ripped to pieces. The storm and towering waves made it impossible for lifeboats to assist in a rescue operation. Survivors were few. The captain, J. M. Jorgensen, attempted to save his small son and wife by strapping the boy to his back and putting a life preserver over his wife's head. Unfortunately, only the captain reached the shore alive.

Many historians claim that Captain Jorgensen could not bear to return to sea for many years after losing his family. But each March for the next thirty-nine years, he did return to the Norwegian Lady to kneel in prayer before the statue and place a bouquet of flowers in the water.

The captain dedicated the rest of his life to the develop-

The Norwegian Lady watches over Virginia Beach shores. (Courtesy Department of Convention and Visitor Development, Virginia Beach)

ment of lifesaving techniques; some are still used today by seafarers. One invention was a lifesaving cask, a round buoy capable of accommodating up to twenty people for a week. The captain toured the world promoting his "lifesaving globe," giving demonstrations of its rescue capabilities. It proved unsinkable when tested during a storm in the English Channel and has since been purchased by many private shipping companies.

The original Norwegian Lady, a figurehead on the ship, was the largest piece of wreckage to reach shore. In the early 1960s, Thomas G. Baptist, who owned a summer home in Virginia Beach, took his children to the statue. The original figure had suffered extensive damage from years of exposure to the strong, salty sea air, so Baptist wrote a letter to the people of Norway about repairing the statue. The people of Moss, Norway, the *Diktator*'s home port, were so moved by Baptist's feeling of loss that they contributed funds for a replacement. Enough money was raised for two statues. The newer nine-foot bronze statue now on display was a gift to the people of Virginia Beach from the people of Moss. An identical statue of the Norwegian Lady is located at the harbor entrance of Moss. The two communities held simultaneous dedication ceremonies to unveil the statues, on September 22, 1962. The original Norwegian Lady mysteriously disappeared and has not been recovered.

Walton's Mountain

Who doesn't remember the television show *The Waltons*, aired on prime-time television during the seventies, and today syndicated as reruns? "Good night, Mary Ellen." "Good night, Elizabeth." "Good night, Grandpa." "Good night, John Boy." With each "Good night," a light in the house turned off. The Waltons represented the American family of the early twentieth century, and millions of viewers loved them. What most of the audience did not know, however, was that the series was based on a real family who lived in Schuyler, Virginia.

Earl Hamner, creator of the popular television series, wrote the show from memories of his own youth. Although the show was filmed at a studio in California, the plots and characters came from Hamner's boyhood life in Schuyler. The Walton boys frequented Rock Fish Gap, Swift Run Gap, Dark Hollow Falls, and Hawksbill, all part of the area around scenic Skyline Drive and Blue Ridge Parkway. The Waltons also visited nearby Charlottesville and Richmond, faraway places by early-twentieth-century standards.

The most famous television mountain, Walton's Mountain, actually does exist, but its real name is Appleberry Mountain. Another popular hangout for John Boy, Jim Bob, and their brothers and sisters is the general store; it still serves the old-fashioned ice cream for which the Walton kids saved their pennies. The elementary school the Walton children attended is also still in use.

Earl Hamner's mother still lives in Schuyler, but you won't find her successful son here too often, as his work keeps him in California.

You can reach Schuyler from Charlottesville by following Route 20 South to Route 6 near Scottsville. Turn right and follow Route 6 to Route 800. Turn left and follow for about 4 miles to Schuyler.

Virginia Wines

Everyone knows that fine wines are made in France, Italy, and California, but Virginia rarely comes to mind! Surprisingly, Virginia has a long tradition of wine production dating from well before California was colonized territory.

Thomas Jefferson wrote: "Wine being among the earliest luxuries in which we indulge ourselves, it is desirable that it should be made here, and we have every soil, aspect, and climate of the best wine countries." Jefferson, the "Father of American Wine," realized incredible potential for making fine wines in Virginia.

America's first wine was produced in 1607 by Jamestown colonists. Today Virginia is the largest wine producer in the eastern United States. Since the 1970s, winemaking in the state has gained in popularity, with total acreage for wine grapes increasing by 420 percent.

In the late 1700s, Filippo Mazzei, an Italian agriculturist, accompanied Jefferson to Virginia and noticed its similarity to the wine regions of France. Mazzei commented in a letter to George Washington: "This country is better calculated than any other I am acquainted with for the production of wine."

In the early nineteenth century, Jefferson planted twenty-three varieties of grapes on his land at Monticello, from imported vines he collected as representative to France from 1784 to 1789. Unfortunately, his crop was destroyed by a small wingless parasite, the phylloxera louse, before he had the chance to harvest it.

Mazzei's judgment was a bit premature, and most believe the best wines in the world are produced elsewhere. The Virginia wine industry did not reach full bloom until the 1970s, when Americans adopted the European custom of regularly drinking wine with meals; the demand for domestic wines skyrocketed. Hundreds of thousands of gallons of wine are now produced at over forty farm wineries in Virginia. Jefferson's dream was secured when the Jeffersonian Wine Grape Growers Society was founded in 1981, dedicated to promoting and supporting wines of Virginia.

Winemakers in Virginia prefer to age their red and white wines in barrels of steel or oak. They typically age white wines for at least a year; red wines are bottled after two.

There are many wine festivals in Virginia, and some wineries are open to the public for tours and tastings. The largest wine festival in the state is the annual Virginia Wineries Association Wine Festival held at the 4-H Center in Front Royal in late June. Highlights are wine and food tastings, crafts, pony rides, and grape stomping. For information write the Virginia Wineries Association, PO Box 96, Barboursville, VA 22923.

Charlottesville, the wine capital of Virginia, is the home of Oakencroft, a winery that offers tastings, tours, and breathtaking panoramic views of the Blue Ridge Mountains in the area around Monticello, where Jefferson tended his private vineyards. Founded in 1978, Oakencroft was first an experimental vineyard but became a commercial operation four years later. The winery has produced gold medal–winning Seyval Blanc, Chardonnay, and Cabernet Sauvignon. At the 1988 summit meeting in Moscow, Ronald Reagan presented an Oakencroft Cabernet Sauvignon to Mikhail Gorbachev. Oakencroft is open for tours and tastings seven days a

111

week (except for holidays) from 11:00 A.M. to 4:00 P.M., April through December. In January through March it is open only on weekends. For more information call (804) 296-4188, weekdays. It is located in Charlottesville, 3.5 miles west on Barracks Road from Route 29.

Jefferson would be proud to know that almost two centuries after his death, his words are still inspiring winegrowers in Virginia. Montdomaine Cellars first planted grapes in the mid-1970s in an area Jefferson suggested in his garden book. Jefferson chose southwestern mountains close to Monticello that offered hillsides with "lean and meager spots of stony and red soil"; he found the area to resemble closely the Burgundy coast, where several famous wines have been produced for centuries. The winery's owners, Mike and Lynn Bowles, scoured the fields of Albemarle County in search of the perfect location. The sixty-acre site

Thomas Jefferson envisaged a perfect grape-growing spot southwest of Monticello, at what is now the Montdomaine Cellars vineyard.
(Photo by Carrie Shook)

they chose, which contains fields that Jefferson originally planted at Mazzei's urging, is now the home of Montdomaine Cellars.

Great care is taken in every process of the winemaking. All grapes are hand-picked, and the fermentation and aging processes are closely monitored. The winery produces 9,000 cases, with a potential of about 20,000, and specializes in Cabernet Sauvignon, Merlot, Chardonnay, and Riesling. With the exception of the Riesling, all wines are matured in French oak for full and rich flavor. The winery has won several gold medals, in the Governor's Cup, Homestead, and Vinifera Wine Growers competitions, among others.

The Montdomaine winery is a few miles south and east of Charlottesville on Route 6. Tours and tastings are held from 10:00 A.M. to 5:00 P.M. daily, April through November. In December through March, the winery is open Monday through Friday, 10:00 A.M. to 5:00 P.M. (weekend tours by appointment only). Call (804) 971-8947 for further information.

Brunswick Stew

Brunswick Stew has been enjoyed by millions since Uncle Jimmy, a black slave and chef, invented it in the early 1800s. On a cold day in 1828, Dr. Creed Haskins of Brunswick County took several of his acquaintances hunting with him, and Jimmy Matthews joined the party as cook for the doctor's hunting expedition.

While the doctor and his friends were out hunting, Uncle Jimmy shot squirrels and prepared them for cooking. This time, though, he decided to try something different, and served a stew instead of the regular roast, to a dubious hunting party. The hunters tasted his mystery stew and were surprised to discover it was wonderful. Second and third helpings were served, and the rest is history!

For the remainder of his life, Uncle Jimmy continued to cook his increasingly famous stew for Dr. Haskins, as well as at community functions and picnics.

After Andrew Jackson won the presidency, the Jeffersonian Party became known as the People's Party. There were many political rallies and the renowned Brunswick stew was always served. Soon the stew became a selling point for rallying more votes, and eventually its popularity spread to neighboring counties and states. Since then, the stew has become "a right good way to raise money," according to Dick Jones, a famous stew master for over thirty years. Perhaps the Democrats should serve up Brunswick stew in 1992!

The original recipe called for squirrels, butter, onions, stale bread, and seasonings. Occasionally, Dr. Haskins would spice it up with a touch of brandy or Madeira. Over time, the recipe has been modified by hundreds of cooks and chicken has replaced squirrel as the meat of choice. However, die-hards insist that if a cook cannot produce a sufficient amount of squirrel, lamb is the only substitute. A descendant of Dr. Haskins insists that the classic version should not include vegetables, which were not in the original Brunswick stew; purists say vegetables should be served only as a side dish. But if you are going to make it at home, put in whatever you like.

When asked for information on their region, most cities and counties send brochures and pamphlets. The county of Brunswick promotes itself by sending a can of specially labeled Brunswick County stew.

In 1988 a legislative session of the General Assembly of the State of Virginia passed House Joint Resolution No. 35, proclaiming Brunswick County the "birthplace of the astonishing gastronomic miracle."

Today, Brunswick stew recipes vary, but the base remains the same: a thick chicken stew, laced heavily with pepper and studded with butter beans and corn. A representative recipe is the following, which will feed an entire family.

Brunswick Stew

  1 qt. water
  1 3-lb. chicken
  2 pieces celery
  1 small onion
  ¼ stick butter
  1 cup chopped onion

115

1 qt. butter beans (fresh is best; frozen or canned will do)
1 qt. whole-kernel corn (fresh, frozen, or canned)
2 qts. (8 cups) tomatoes
3 medium potatoes, diced
salt, red pepper, black pepper (to taste)
bread crumbs, crackers, or biscuits (optional)

Place the water in a large pot and simmer the chicken with the celery and onion until meat is tender (about 45 minutes). Cool. Discard celery, and shred meat from bones and return to pot.

Add remaining ingredients and continue cooking over medium heat for at least 5 hours. Add water if necessary and stir occasionally until thick. Season with salt, red pepper, and more black pepper to taste. Thicken with bread crumbs, crackers, or biscuit crumbs. Serves 4 to 6.

Methods vary, and some cooks add okra, diced carrots, beef, and/or sugar. There are still a few who add "a little old brandy for flavor," as Creed Haskins did in the old days. Whatever variations you might try, it is still Uncle Jimmy's famous Brunswick stew from Brunswick County, Virginia.

The Virginians

The United States owes a great deal to four Virginians who actually created the country we know today. When independence from Great Britain was only a dream, there were a few who thought it could be a reality. Several early leaders from Virginia, including George Washington, Thomas Jefferson, James Madison, and James Monroe, envisioned a successful independent nation, and each contributed a great deal to make it a reality. These four native Virginians went on to become the earliest presidents.

George Washington

The first president of the United States, the "Father of Our Country" was a living legend who threw a silver dollar across the Potomac and who as a boy would never tell a lie.

Washington was born on a plantation in Westmoreland County on February 22, 1732. His family moved to Truro Parish when he was three and to Ferry Farm, near Fredericksburg, when he was seven. Four years later his father died and he went to live with his older half-brother, Lawrence, at Mount Vernon.

Washington did not have a formal education, but he acquired a license to be a public surveyor. At the age of twenty, on November 6, 1752, Washington became one of four adjutant generals of the Virginia militia. He attained the rank of major and received a salary of $500 a year. After two years he was promoted to lieutenant colonel, but he resigned from military service later that year.

Washington became famous as an aide-de-camp to British general Edward Braddock. On July 9, 1755, as Braddock and his army were approaching the French Fort Duquesne (present-day Pittsburgh), they were ambushed by the French and Indians. Washington, ill with a high fever, was forced to ride into the battle with a pillow rather than a saddle. Two horses were shot out from under him; his jacket was ripped by four more bullets. Braddock's contingent was defeated. The general was killed, and Washington helped carry him from the battlefield. His brave leadership earned him a promotion to colonel and commander in chief of all the colony's troops.

In 1759, he married a wealthy widow, Martha Custis. They had no children of their own, but Washington adopted her two children, Jacky and Patsy, and also Jacky's children, Eleanor Parke Custis and George Washington Parke Custis, after their father's death.

After one defeat, Washington was elected to the House of Burgesses on July 24, 1758. He then started his active part in the disputes that gradually brought the colonies to war with England. Washington was one of the first leaders in the colonies to fight for independence from Great Britain.

The respect he received from the colonists led to his appointment by the Second Continental Congress as commander in chief of all colonial forces, on June 15, 1775. The Revolutionary War came to a close in the fall of 1781, when Washington and the French forces surrounded General Cornwallis's British troops at Yorktown and forced them to surrender. Two years later, the British signed the Treaty of Paris that recognized American independence.

Washington returned to Mount Vernon hoping to lead the life of a private citizen. His retirement did not last long; in 1787 he was chosen by the Constitutional Convention to be its presiding officer. When a constitution for the new government was adopted and accepted by the new states, Washington was voted unanimously the nation's first president. Although he would have preferred to stay at Mount Vernon, his strong sense of duty forced him to accept. On April 30, 1789, he was inaugurated president, with John Adams as vice-president.

By the end of his second term, Washington refused to consider a third. He wrote his farewell address with Alexander Hamilton's aid and delivered it on September 19,

1796. In it he urged his countrymen to remain true to their ideals and to avoid the evils that would endanger the safety of the Union. Adams was elected to succeed as president, and Washington finally returned to his home.

At Mount Vernon, he worked the fields and took care of the plantation. In early December 1799, he caught a bad cold that developed into an acute condition, making his breathing difficult. His doctor used the traditional method of "bleeding" (drawing blood from his body) several times. Washington became weaker and weaker, and died on December 14, 1799.

The first census, taken at the time of his death, revealed various figures about the new nation he had helped develop: There were almost 4,000,000 citizens, most of them farmers. Only 1 in 20 lived in a town. Only five cities along the Atlantic coast had populations of over 10,000; the largest of these was New York City, with 33,000 inhabitants.

Thomas Jefferson

The third president of the United States wrote a brief summary of his own accomplishments, for his epitaph: "Here was buried Thomas Jefferson, author of the Declaration of Independence, of the statute of Virginia for religious freedom, and father of the University of Virginia." This, by any standard, is a very brief encapsulation of his career, as he made many more valuable contributions to his state and to the people of the United States.

Jefferson was born on April 13, 1743, the son of a wealthy planter at Shadwell in Albemarle County. When his father died, fourteen-year-old Thomas inherited a large estate. He was educated at the College of William and Mary in Williamsburg, where he studied the sciences. He continued at the college after graduation, and under the supervision of George Wythe, the first professor of law in the country, Jefferson prepared to be a lawyer.

At twenty-six, he began constructing a home on the highest hill of his estate near Charlottesville. He continued improving his plantation, Monticello, for the next twenty-five years, using his skills as an architect, engineer, and landscape artist.

In 1772 Jefferson married Martha Wayles Skelton. In the ten years of their marriage Martha bore six children, but only two daughters reached maturity. Jefferson and his wife had a very happy marriage until Martha's death, on

September 6, 1782. Jefferson grieved for many months and never remarried.

Jefferson, who inherited his father's position as justice of the peace, had a strong interest in politics. He was appointed by the governor of Virginia as militia commander for Albemarle County in 1770 and served in the Virginia House of Burgesses from 1769 to 1775, when he began his work against British rule. Jefferson was a delegate to the Second Continental Congress in 1775 and 1776. When Congress adopted a resolution in 1776 asking the colonies to form new governments, a resolution for independence was also passed. In June of that year, Congress chose a committee to write the new declaration and named Jefferson chairman. Although he was only thirty-three, he had a reputation for writing well and was appointed to draft the declaration. The Declaration of Independence, written mostly by Jefferson, was adopted by Congress on July 4, 1776.

Jefferson was elected to the state legislature in 1776. During his three years of service, he wrote several important laws. The most important one provided for the separation of church and state which became one of the foundations of freedom in the United States. His work in the legislature led to his election as governor of Virginia in June 1779.

In June 1783 the Virginia legislature elected Jefferson to the Congress of the Confederation. On May 7, 1784, he was instructed to go to Europe to make trade agreements. He assisted Benjamin Franklin and John Adams, and remained for five years. When Franklin retired in 1785, Jefferson became minister to France.

Jefferson returned to the United States and served as secretary of state under Washington for nearly four years beginning in 1790. In 1796, Jefferson ran against John Adams for the presidency. Adams won with an electoral vote of 71 to 68 and Jefferson became vice-president. He was elected president in 1800, closely defeating Aaron Burr.

The Rotunda designed by Thomas Jefferson at the University of Virginia in Charlottesville. (Photo by Carrie Shook)

Jefferson's first administration was a huge success. He reduced the public debt and ended unpopular taxes. The most important event of his first term was the purchase of the Louisiana Territory in 1803. Jefferson commissioned the Lewis and Clark Expedition to explore the new territory from 1804 to 1806. He was reelected in 1804, but his second term was not as successful. Jefferson failed to purchase Florida from Spain, and he approved the Embargo Act of

1807, which, while it cut off exports to Great Britain and France, struck a crippling blow to the economy. The loss of so much business to American farmers, merchants, shipowners, and seamen forced Jefferson to repeal the act just before he left office.

After forty years in public office, Jefferson retired to his beloved Monticello. He spent the rest of his life working in the gardens and on the house, and pursuing scientific theories and inventions. His most important work in these years was the establishment of the University of Virginia. He designed the buildings, planned the curriculum, chose the faculty, and selected the books. The university opened in 1825 and is still one of the greatest institutions of higher education in the country.

Both Jefferson and John Adams died on July 4, 1826, the fiftieth anniversary of the Declaration of Independence.

James Madison

James Madison was born on March 16, 1751, in Port Conway. A frail child, he grew to only five feet tall. As the eldest child in his family, he was given an excellent education and attended the College of New Jersey (now Princeton).

Madison began his long career in politics as chairman of the Committee of Public Safety for Orange County in 1775. The next year he was elected to the Virginia Convention, the legislative body. In 1779 he began his term in the Continental Congress, where he worked out a compromise plan for states with claims to land west of Pennsylvania and north of Ohio. This land became the Northern Territory. He also made an agreement with the Spanish that allowed farmers in the West to ship goods down the Mississippi River. When his term ended in 1783, he returned to Montpelier for a year. In 1784 he was elected to the Virginia House of Delegates, where he worked for religious freedom and helped defeat tax support for churches.

As a member of the Virginia Delegation to the Constitutional Convention, he led a group that called for a much stronger central government. Many of Madison's proposals became the foundation for the Constitution of the United States, and helped write the final draft of the Constitution more clearly and concisely. Madison is now known as the "Father of the Constitution" because of his great contributions. Essays Madison wrote on the Constitution, collected as

The Federalist, are among the most important explanations of the Constitution and the political theory on which it is based.

In 1794, at the age of forty-three, Madison married Dolly Payne Todd, a twenty-six-year-old mother and widow. He succeeded his close friend Thomas Jefferson as president in 1809, having defeated Federalist C. C. Pinckney, and served two consecutive terms. In 1812 Madison asked Congress for a declaration of war against the British (this was the War of 1812). During the second year of Madison's second term, British troops stormed Washington, D.C. and set fire to the city. The Madisons were forced to leave the White House but Dolly was able to save several personal possessions, papers, and a large portrait of George Washington by Gilbert Stuart.

After serving as president, Madison retired to Montpelier, where he remained until he died, on June 28, 1836. He was buried on the grounds there.

James Monroe

The fifth president of the United States, James Monroe was born on April 28, 1758, in Westmoreland County. In 1774 Monroe began attending the College of William and Mary; he studied there until 1776, when he was commissioned a lieutenant in the Third Virginia Regiment.

On Christmas Day, 1776, Monroe was wounded at the Battle of Trenton; he was cited by General George Washington for bravery. After spending a winter at Valley Forge with the Continental Army, he earned the rank of lieutenant colonel. He won fame in the Revolutionary War, and appears holding the American flag in the painting *Washington Crossing the Delaware*.

Following the advice of his mentor Thomas Jefferson, Monroe studied law and established a law practice in Fredericksburg. In his long career of public service he held more offices than any other president. He was a U.S. senator; minister to France, to Spain, and to England; governor of Virginia; and the only man to hold simultaneously the offices of secretary of war and secretary of state. Monroe is also the only president to run unopposed for president besides Washington.

Monroe accomplished many important missions while serving the country. In 1803 he completed negotiations for the Louisiana Purchase with the French. He also arranged for the release of Thomas Paine, the famous colonist known for his motivating pamphlets, who was imprisoned in France in 1792.

The period in which he served as president is referred to as the Era of Good Feelings. Monroe is best remembered for his 1823 address to Congress, in which he presented the outline of the principles of the Monroe Doctrine.

Monroe was the first president to hold his inauguration out of doors, on March 4, 1817. This custom survives today, as do many other practices introduced by the Monroes. First Lady Elizabeth Kortright Monroe was the first to introduce a formal style of entertaining official guests at the White House. Maria, their daughter, was the first president's daughter to have a White House wedding, and the Monroes were the first family to live in the new White House.

The original pink sandstone structure was burned by the British during the War of 1812. The outer walls, which had been heavily smoke-stained, were covered by a fresh coat of white paint. This is how the White House acquired its name. Many of the rooms still contain French furniture the Monroes imported from Europe.

Monroe planned to spend his retirement with his family at the home he built, Highland, in the Charlottesville area. The Monroes lived there for twenty-five years, until 1825, when debts forced Monroe to sell his beloved farm. He died at his youngest daughter's home in New York City on July 4, 1831, the third president (after Adams and Jefferson) to die on Independence Day. His body was originally buried in New York City, but in 1858 his remains were transferred to Hollywood Cemetery in Richmond.